An Infinity of Graces

CECIL ROSS PINSENT, AN ENGLISH ARCHITECT IN THE ITALIAN LANDSCAPE

Ethne Clarke

W. W. NORTON & COMPANY

NEW YORK • LONDON

For information about permission to reproduce
selections from this book, write to
Permissions, W. W. Norton & Company, Inc.,
500 Fifth Avenue, New York, NY 10110

For information about special discounts for bulk
purchases, please contact W. W. Norton Special Sales
at specialsales@wwnorton.com or 800-233-4830

Manufacturing by Walsworth Print Group
Book design by Jonathan D. Lippincott
Production manager: Leeann Graham

Library of Congress Cataloging-in-Publication Data

Clarke, Ethne.
An infinity of graces : Cecil Ross Pinsent, an English
architect in the Italian landscape / Ethne Clarke. — 1st ed.
    p. cm.
Cecil Ross Pinsent, an English architect in the Italian landscape
Includes bibliographical references and index.
ISBN 978-0-393-73221-4 (hardcover)
1. Pinsent, Cecil, 1884–1963. 2. Landscape architects—Italy—
History—20th century. 3. Landscape design—Italy—History—
20th century. I. Title. II. Title: Cecil Ross Pinsent, an English
architect in the Italian landscape.
SB469.386.I8C57 2013
712.0945—dc23
                                        2013001562

W. W. Norton & Company, Inc.,
500 Fifth Avenue, New York, N.Y. 10110
www.wwnorton.com

W. W. Norton & Company Ltd., Castle House,
75/76 Wells Street, London W1T 3QT

1 2 3 4 5 6 7 8 9 0

Here I sit for the first time in the enchanted air in which love and faith and art and knowledge are warranted to become deeper passions than in my own chilly clime. I begin to behold the promise of my dreams. It's Italy.

—Henry James, *At Isella* (1871)

Contents

Preface

Though separated by nearly a century, Cecil Pinsent and I have a lot in common. We were both expatriates for thirty years, he an Englishman who lived in Italy for three decades in the early part of the twentieth century, I an American who made England my home for the last thirty years of the same century. Pinsent built his career in his adopted home, as did I, but while Pinsent came to feel more at ease in Italy than in England, I eventually tired of always being the foreigner. It may well have been this feeling of being an outsider that fostered in me a longing to understand the hows and whys of belonging, and to explore the way expatriates have influenced the arts in their host countries. It certainly is what fired my curiosity about earlier expatriates—like Edith Wharton, the Pulitzer Prize–winning American novelist who settled in France (and for her refugee work during World War I was given the Légion d'honneur), or Henry James, whose novels depicting the collisions between new American money and the entrenched sensibilities of the British class structure gave rise to the term "Henry James Americans." Virginian Nancy Lancaster transformed the aesthetic of English country house interior design by grafting onto it American ideals of easy elegance and comfort, while Lawrence Johnston, whose family came from old New York stock, made his home at Hidcote Manor, in Gloucestershire, and developed a garden there that became the model for a style that is now recognized the world over as the English cottage garden.

Because we expatriates come to our adopted homes unfettered by ideas of what is "proper," it may be that we are more able to absorb and express the essence of a place. But when I arrived in Florence in 1986, I gazed out over the landscape in awe and ignorance. It was my first visit, made in the mold of the Grand Tour, but rather than travel with a retinue in a horse-drawn carriage, I was with my husband and six-year-old son in the family Volkswagen. On a self-guided tour to expand my knowledge of garden history, I arrived clutching my copy of Georgina Masson's 1961 classic, *Italian Gardens*, along with Wharton's *Italian Villas and Their Gardens*, and I managed to visit the high points. Villa Gamberaia, with its garden plan a perfect progression from light to dark, rustic to classical, left me speechless—and at my first sight of its famous water parterre I burst into tears. The Villa Medici at Fiesole made me curious to learn more about the history of Italian gardens, because from its tiny *giardino segreto* (secret garden), a true relic of the Renaissance, I glimpsed another, even more charming garden; I later learned that it was Villa Le Balze, one of Pinsent's earliest Florentine gardens.

That visit laid the foundations for my book *The Gardens of Tuscany* and introduced me to Sir Harold Acton. We met in the salon of his home, Villa La Pietra. He sat in a rather dilapidated wing chair that was covered in faded silk damask; I perched on an armchair into which, in a more relaxed frame of mind, I might easily have slouched. Sir Harold was graciousness personified. I was tongue-tied. But then, serendipitously, I mentioned that I was originally from Park Forest, Illinois. "But my mother came from Evanston!" he exclaimed. "I used to visit there regularly as a child, and adored Marshall Field's." So two expatriates found common ground, exchanging reminiscences about the store's famed restaurant, the Walnut Room.

During the interview, Sir Harold described how his father, Arthur Acton, designed the garden surrounding the Villa La Pietra to be a showcase for his immense collection of classical sculpture. He mentioned that his father had consulted Cecil Pinsent about the addition of a small garden building at the villa, a project never pursued. Pinsent, he explained, was the architect of many of the villas and landscapes built by the Anglo-American community, which included some of the most notable members of the expatriate literati in Florence, and these villas and gardens were today among the most admired in Tuscany. Sir Harold brought his palms together as if in prayer, and resting his chin on delicately poised fingertips, fixed me with a steady gaze. "You know," he said, "you really ought to find out everything you can about Pinsent. So little about him is known with any accuracy." When someone of Sir Harold's stature makes a suggestion, you're well advised to listen.

Returning to my home in Norfolk, I did what research I could on Pinsent and included the lean results in *The Gardens of Tuscany*, published in 1990 with a foreword by Sir Harold. But with his words of advice about Pinsent lingering in the back of my mind, I began to look for primary sources of information. I started with the Royal Institute of British Architects; as Pinsent had been a RIBA Fellow this seemed an obvious source—but not as useful, I was to discover, as the daily newspaper I read.

One of the most enjoyable sections of *The Times*, London's most venerable daily, is Letters to the Editor. Reading through this correspondence one morning, not too long after the publication of the Tuscan garden book, I came upon a letter from Sir Christopher Pinsent, noted British sculptor and Royal Academician. I wrote to him that day inquiring if Cecil Pinsent was, by any chance, one of his relatives. He responded immediately, giving me the address of Pinsent's niece, Chloe Morton, who had in her possession all that remained of Pinsent's archive of drawings and photographs. I visited Mrs. Morton, who enthusiastically embraced my purpose and lent me the archive to catalog, study, and photograph so that I could one day use the contents to illustrate a book on Pinsent's life and work.

The fact that my research has taken so many years turns out to have had its advantages. In early 2011, not long after I had submitted what I hoped would be the final draft of the manuscript, I had a letter from Helen Morton, Chloe's daughter and Pinsent's great-niece. Six more photo albums had come into her possession, and would I like to see them? I owe a special debt of gratitude to Helen Morton for loaning me these valuable albums, which reveal much about Pinsent's creative process. Chloe Morton also introduced me to Basil Pinsent, Cecil's half-brother (by his father's second marriage) and his younger sibling by more than twenty-five years, who remembered him with the greatest affection and, it must be said, amusement. A sense of humor was not far below the surface of either brother, I came to learn. Basil, who died before this book was completed, was able to provide me with much firsthand information about Pinsent's inquisitive nature and method of working. I find it hard to express how much I appreciate the generosity of these kind people.

In 1998 I received a Cline Fellowship from the Harry Ransom Humanities Research Center at the University of Texas at Austin. This grant helped fund a one-year period of research in the center's collections, which include a few Berenson papers as well as letters, diaries, and published works of literary figures who, in writing about their experiences of culture and travel in Florence and Tuscany during the nineteenth and early twentieth centuries, helped to illuminate for me the popular idea of life *all'italiana*.

David Ottewill provided copies of his correspondence with Iris Origo on the subject of Pinsent. Nigel Nicolson gave me access to his family archive held at Sissinghurst Castle, Kent, and allowed me to read and transcribe the letters from Geoffrey Scott to Vita Sackville-West. The librarian and staff of the Fototeca at Villa I Tatti – The Harvard University Center for Italian Renaissance Studies have been helpful beyond measure and generous in their welcome, facilitating my research, sometimes at a moment's notice; I especially acknowledge the support and friendship of Michael Rocke, Fiorella Superbi, and Allen Grieco, who have been as curious as I about Pinsent and his relationship with the Berensons. Similarly, the staff at Le Balze, Georgetown University's study center in Florence, has welcomed me on numerous occasions.

I've made many visits to the sites of Pinsent's most significant projects, frequently with writers, researchers, and fellow garden

From childhood, Pinsent and his brothers were keen photographers. Here, Pinsent is shown photographing his brother Gerry, who is the one photographing Pinsent: a souvenir of their journey through Italy in 1935. The nine albums that survive describe a chronology of Pinsent's life: his family, friends, lovers, and travels. But they also provide insight into his working methods, his varied sources of inspiration, and his villas and gardens, among which I Tatti, Le Balze, La Foce, and Gli Scafari are the ones given most attention.

historians and designers. Most important to me were the visits I made with Professor Giorgio Galletti, a Florentine architect and leading authority on Italian garden history; I greatly benefited from his shared scholarship and friendship. Giorgio published a paper in 1991, quoted in this book, which I first read in translation in 1994, before we met for the first time at La Foce. After meeting me at a café in Chianciano Terme, Giorgio took me to La Foce, where we linked up with Alessandro Tombelli, the head gardener there at the time. So began my garden connection with these good men and the place, as Alessandro, too, has been a guide, mentor, and most valued friend since our first contact at

La Foce. I am especially grateful to Marchesa Benedetta Origo for welcoming me to La Foce on so many occasions. Most recently she sat me comfortably at her own desk in the villa so that I could study a small collection of Pinsent's jocular verse written for her mother, Iris Origo; those words brought their relationship more clearly into focus. Benedetta's own book, *La Foce: A Garden and Landscape in Tuscany*, is an eloquent tribute to her parents' untiring work to better the lives of the *mezzadri*, the sharecroppers who helped the couple build a fertile farm and—at times—sanctuary from the unyielding *crete*, or native clay soil, of the Val d'Orcia. I am indebted to the other villa and garden owners who assisted me with my research, as well as all those who kindly consented to be interviewed, and I ask their indulgence for not listing them by name; to do so would take many more pages than I am allowed.

My thanks run long and deep to them and to all the people who have supported me during the lengthy period of research that became this book. Not least among them is Professor Vincent Shacklock, senior academic in the school of art, architecture, and design at the University of Lincoln. We met at the first, and so far only, conference dedicated to Pinsent's life and work, held at Villa Le Balze in 1995 and sponsored by Georgetown University. In 1995 I had reached a point in my research where I felt I needed to stop or find a very good reason to continue; Professor Shacklock, then in the School of Conservation Studies at De Montfort University, Leicester, gave me that reason when he offered me the opportunity to continue my research in a postgraduate degree program.

•

This book has taken me on a long journey. Along the way I have met many wonderful, helpful people, whose encouragement has spurred me on as I followed all the tangential byways that so often map a person's life. These tangents have led me to reconsider elements of Pinsent's life and the times in which he worked, and even, I have to say, my own life and the direction it has taken. I would like to express my deepest thanks to Tom Romich, who, when I told him I was hoping to publish a book on Pinsent, mentioned it to Nancy Green, editor of architecture books at W. W. Norton. It has taken a good deal longer than either of us planned to come to press. But decades between works seem to suit the subjects, as like gardens they need to fill out. I am grateful to Nancy for her vision and her *pazienza*. I once remarked to her that it has been my wont to research the lives of the obscure and little known and to produce slight works that may gather their subjects some notice. I'm glad to say that Pinsent's turn has finally come.

An Infinity
of Graces

Introduction:
Notions of Italy

When today's visitors first encounter the charm and elegance of Cecil Pinsent's Florentine villas and gardens, they see what they want to see—Renaissance beauty—not recognizing that they are admiring the work of a twentieth-century English architect. At a time when architects on both sides of the Atlantic were building country places and manor houses *in the style* of the Italian Renaissance, Pinsent was working where that style originated. His clients were cultured, well-educated people steeped in the art and history of the Renaissance, and consequently less willing than nouveau-riche industrialists to be gulled by pastiche. As he built or renovated villas and gardens in the hills around Florence, his peers increasingly recognized him as an adept in the architectural and landscape language of the Italian Renaissance. And he was generous in sharing his expertise; Pinsent escorted many young architects around Florence. The landscape architect Sir Geoffrey Jellicoe recalled spending time with Pinsent in 1923 when he was in Florence drawing and measuring villas and gardens. He and a companion spent an entire day with Pinsent, walking the hills of Fiesole; as Jellicoe described it, "Pinsent was very sensitive to landscape, and he became my first maestro in the art of placing buildings in the landscape." Jellicoe's remark pays tribute to Pinsent's understanding of the genius loci and his sensitivity to the needs of his clients and the needs of the buildings and landscapes he was called upon to create.

•

From the mid-eighteenth century Italy in general, and Florence in particular, had been the prime destination for Anglo-American cultural, economic, and social refugees. Edmund and Mary Houghton, who took the twenty-two-year-old Pinsent on an extended tour of Tuscany and encouraged him to set up an architectural practice there, were expatriates of some years' standing, their impetus being economic and cultural. Edmund Houghton was a solicitor, but he did not practice, preferring instead to live an aesthete's life, supported by a small private income and surrounded by fine antiques, in which he traded part-time. The cost of living in Italy during the eighteenth and most of the nineteenth centuries was considerably less than in either the United Kingdom or, especially, the United States, where devaluation in the aftermath of the Civil War meant the dollar stretched much further abroad than it did at home. Many "old money" U.S. citizens spent months at a time living in Europe while renting out their family's city mansions or country estates to the "new money" industrial tycoons. Often the months abroad turned into years, and it was just these people who came to be known as "Henry James Americans."

Others came for their health; tuberculosis was a common ailment afflicting people of every social class, and the mild Italian climate was deemed more beneficial than that of anywhere else in Europe save the Côte d'Azur. Many English expatriates, as well as Americans who sought a more cultured surrounding than could be found at sanitariums in the Catskills or the American South or Southwest, chose to live in Italy for the sake of their health. Florence in the early 1900s was a cultural magnet for writers, artists, philosophers, musicians, and dancers, who were attracted by the city's artistic heritage. But for many, the attraction of Florence as the cradle of the Renaissance and of humanist culture provided the greatest draw. The city was perceived as a place where one could indulge the notion of a romantic life, civilized by the pursuit of intellectual and personal freedom, away from the hidebound and stultifying expectations and constraints imposed by the rigid social systems of northern Europe, Britain, and North America. It was this milieu that supplied the background and often the plot for many novels of the period, notably those of Edith Wharton and Henry James.

Florence was particularly attractive to English and American visitors, guided in their appreciation by John Ruskin's book *Mornings in Florence* (1875–77), subtitled "Written for the Help of the Few Who Still Care for Her Monuments," or following the Baedeker guide (the Frommer's or Michelin guide of the era), as did Pinsent, who carried the Italian-language edition in order to learn architectural terminology. For such visitors the ancient villas, palazzos, small rural chapels, and walled hilltop villages were the ideal emotional and physical environment, the complete antithesis of the polluted northern European and North American cities of the Industrial Age.

Even then, however, Florence was changing under the modernizing schemes of urban improvers like Ubaldino Peruzzi, the mayor of Florence who, in 1870, taking Baron Haussmann's contemporaneous modernization of Paris as his model, caused the fourteenth-century city walls to be razed and long, straight, broad avenues or *viali* to be superimposed on the random network of medieval alleyways and narrow streets that divided Florence into enclaves based on the palazzos of the great Renaissance families. Henry James, in his guide *Italian Hours,* began the chapter on Florence with a complaint about the modernizing process that was altering the character of the city, and he remarked unfavorably too on the numbers of tourists. But he concluded that enough remained to satisfy the seeker of the "old Florence." He wrote, "On the north side of the Arno, between Ponte Vecchio and Ponte Santa Trinità, is a row of immemorial houses that back on the river, in whose yellow flood they bathe their sore old feet. Anything more battered and befouled, more cracked and disjointed, dirtier, drearier, poorer, it would be impossible to conceive."

Yet this is the quintessential scene that James was sure the "infatuated alien" would find alluring. Commenting on his admiration for Florentine domestic architecture, James referred specifically to the "large serious faces" of the palaces along the via dei Bardi, adding, "The merchant nobles of the fifteenth century had deep and full pockets, I suppose, though the present bearers of their names are glad to let out their palaces in suites of apartments which are occupied by the commercial aristocracy of another republic." Indeed, Edmund and Mary Houghton occupied an apartment in one such building—it and nearly all of its neighbors were destroyed by heavy bombing during World War II, as can be seen in Pinsent's photographs of the area, appearing later in this book.

One of the earliest popularizers of Italian gardens and villas was Edith Wharton, whose book *Italian Villas and Their Gardens* was published in 1904 with illustrations by the fashionable American watercolorist Maxfield Parrish. As Wharton was part of Bernard and Mary Berenson's circle, the Houghtons were probably familiar with her and her work and would have urged their protégé to study it before setting off for Italy. Wharton's book was notable as the first to examine the Italian garden as a work of art and the first to provide an in-depth history of the most important examples around Italy. (The American architect Charles Platt had published a book on Italian villas and gardens a decade earlier, but his was primarily an appreciation, illustrated with artistically composed black-and-white photographs, with scant explanatory text.)

Wharton's travels in and around Italy in the years 1902 and 1903 were guided in part by the writings of Vernon Lee, the nom de plume of Violet Paget, an English expatriate living in Florence. Paget wrote on aesthetics and art appreciation, but she also wrote the sort of romanticized Italian travel musings that were a popular companion to the practical Baedeker guides most tourists followed. Wharton's own perception of Italy was heavily influenced by her admiration of Paget, whom she had met on an earlier trip. On her arrival at the Hotel Bristol in Florence in early March 1903, Wharton wrote to a friend: "Miss Paget has such a prodigious list of villas for me to see near here and is taking so much trouble to arrange expeditions for us that I think we shall have to stay here longer than I expected . . . [Paget's] long familiarity with the Italian countryside, and the wide circle of her Italian friendships, made it easy for her to guide me to all the right places and put me in relation with people who could enable me to visit them . . . [W]herever I went I found open doors." A month later Wharton wrote to Paget, "No one has your gift of suggesting in a few touches an Italian landscape or picture," and she praised Paget's writings for awakening her appreciation of the "despised, foolish and brilliant eighteenth century in Italy, which no one saw till you told us to look."

Tourists gave most of their attention to art, landscape, and architecture, but their contact and interaction with native Florentines was minimal, as they generally kept their distance from the local population. Where there was contact, efforts were made to make the Italians seem less "foreign"; female staff at the *pensioni* or hotels were often dressed in the uniforms of English parlor maids. As early as 1847 an English-language newspaper was being published in Florence. In the 1860s the British journalist George Augustus Sala commented that Florence was a hybrid city, "where English boarding houses elbow Italian *locandas* [inns]; English bakers sell you captain's biscuits and poundcakes; and Dr. Broomback's Academy for the Sons of Gentlemen is within twenty minutes' walk of the Pitti Palace." (Pinsent's first lodgings were located in this Anglo-American enclave, in a small pensione on the via dei Seragli, even closer to the Pitti than Dr. Broomback's, and not far from the hallowed halls of the Brownings' apartments, the Casa Guidi on the Piazza San Felice, across the street from the Pitti Palace.)

The late English novelist and social historian Sir Malcolm Bradbury, writing of the American response to abroad, describes the perception that dirt, disease, beggars, tricksters, and "bands of swarthy gesticulating foreigners" lay in wait to defraud the unwary traveler. Despite the use of phrase books, language remained a barrier—as Bradbury notes, citing Mark Twain's remark in *Cruise of the Quaker City:* "We never did succeed in making those idiots understand their own language." This and Twain's other humorous and sometimes cynical observations on foreign travel, as in *Innocents Abroad,* shaped the attitudes of many English-speaking travelers to Europe.

Lured by guidebooks, travel articles in the popular press, and novels and poetry lauding the marvels of Italy, visitors' and expatriate residents' contradictory attitudes were shaped by the literary response to that country. For example, the lifestyle of the simple country folk was romanticized and idealized, yet standards of hygiene and accommodation were a constant source of complaint. The natives were admired, yet at the same time regarded as shiftless and basically untrustworthy—although when held in comparison to their English or American counterparts, who were perceived as boorish, the natives were deemed to be cultured, civilized, and dependable. Medical care in Italy was deeply suspect, yet the climate, spas, and lifestyle were thought to be the most healthful for those already weakened by disease. The Catholic religion was deprecated as a system of superstition and hocus-pocus, yet the native population owed their integrity to their unquestioning adherence to this strict system of religious belief. Most astonishing, perhaps, the art and architecture that was so often the focus of visitors' admiration was perceived to be falling into dereliction because the natives did not care for it or understand the importance of their national art treasures. Only the cultured Anglo-American travelers were, they themselves thought, able to appreciate these aspects of Italian life, and this is what made it permissible for them to export major artworks and entire sections of important buildings to their estates in Britain and America. Houghton, the antique collector, and Bernard Berenson, the connoisseur, were to some extent guilty of this arrogance as they pursued the acquisition of Italian artifacts on behalf of clients; Pinsent would certainly have been aware of this practice, if not himself party to it. Today, as the move to return misappropriated cultural artifacts to their countries of origin continues to gain traction, we view the matter differently, but from the Gilded Age until well after the Second World War, it was business as usual.

•

Into this contradictory milieu stepped Cecil Pinsent, who never actively sought recognition or acclaim. Until relatively recently little had been written on Pinsent and, most significantly, what there was tended to cast him in the shadow of his business partner, Geoffrey Scott, or, on the most cursory study, dismiss his work as "pastiche."

In 1983 Erika Neubauer, an Austrian garden historian, published the first major article in English on Pinsent, although it is limited to a discussion of his landscape work supported by a list of the gardens he designed, drawn from his own client inventory. Another writer who has touched on Pinsent and his landscape work is the English architectural historian David Ottewill, who presents a balanced discussion and accurate account of Pinsent's work set within its historical context in his book *The Edwardian Garden* (1988). In his 1992 book *The English Garden Abroad*, the English garden-writer Charles Quest-Ritson includes an account of Pinsent and his work at I Tatti and La Foce. An article by another English garden-writer, Patrick Bowe's "Designs on Tuscan Soil," describes the gardens at La Foce and provides a sketch of Pinsent's career and association with Geoffrey Scott.

Popular writers such as Quest-Ritson and Bowe, when describing the partnership of Pinsent and Scott, often cast Scott as having equal role in the venture, chiefly on the strength of Scott's enduring book *The Architecture of Humanism* (first published in 1914). Some remarks by the English art historian Sir Kenneth Clark in his memoir, *Another Part of the Wood*, also cast Scott as Pinsent's equal in their brief working relationship; Clark also suggests that Pinsent was homosexual. In fact there is no documentation to support either supposition; quite the contrary in fact. Richard Dunn, Scott's biographer, promotes the idea of Scott as a practicing and influential architect, but as his biography shows, Scott made only brief attempts to obtain a formal architectural education.

In 1995 a symposium on Pinsent's life and work was held at Villa Le Balze, sponsored by Georgetown University. It examined his biography (my contribution to the proceedings) but also included Giorgio Galletti's investigation of Pinsent's recorded works in Tuscany and other papers that described the restoration of and conservation outlook for Italian gardens; particular consideration was given to the history of Villa Le Balze and a conservation master plan for the site, developed by Vincent Shacklock and the School of Conservation Study at De Montfort University, Leicester, England. Since then, there have been a few articles published on Pinsent, including several that I've written. The English landscape architect Peter Curzon has assisted Benedetta Origo with sensitive renovations of the La Foce gardens, and Pinsent's name is appearing as a draw on tours of Tuscan gardens.

As the biographer of one of architecture's rather obscure practitioners, it was fortunate for me that several of Pinsent's more notable clients, many of whom remained lifelong friends, were inveterate letter-writers and memoirists. Their autobiographies and collected letters, as well as published biographies and extensive archival material, particularly the Berenson papers at I Tatti, are useful in establishing not only the identities of the people with whom Pinsent was involved, but also the milieu in which he found himself. Pinsent never felt compelled to write down the story of his life, and he kept little in the way of letters or business records—indeed, I was told that he was a methodically tidy man who in his retirement discarded a portion of his possessions every three years. But in 1955, while preparing a review (never published) of his work for *Country Life* magazine in collaboration with the arts journalist John Fraser, Pinsent compiled a list of his clients and projects, both built and unbuilt. That list, together with the nine albums of photographs and drawings that represent all that Pinsent thought worth saving and reveal much about his creative process, enable us to develop a sound sense of the man and his work, and open a window onto a time when architecture and the arts were moving from the Golden Age to the Modern period—a move that, as we will see, caused Pinsent no little disappointment.

ONE

Shaping a Language of Design

Cecil Pinsent once wrote to his longtime friend and mentor, Bernard Berenson, that so many of the good things that happen during one's life happen purely by accident. He had in mind his arrival in Florence in 1907, but fate, as always, had a hand in many of the little twists that shaped his life.

Pinsent was born an expatriate, on May 5, 1884, in Montevideo, Uruguay. He was the third of four children, all born in that city. His mother, Alice Mary (née Nuttal), the daughter of an English expatriate family in South America, met his father, Ross Pinsent, through family friends, and they were married in England in 1877. Not long afterward the couple returned to South America, where Ross had already established himself as an entrepreneurial businessman and where he continued to develop his import/export enterprises and investments in the continent's growing railroad industries.

Montevideo, a prosperous port and cosmopolitan city on the Rio Plata, rivaled Buenos Aires in its importance as a cultural center, and in the expatriate community the Pinsent family maintained a position as members of upper-middle-class Victorian society. From Pinsent's photo album it is clear that they were frequent visitors to the home of T. D. Lawrie, a family friend and a substantial landowner. His ranch, the Estancia Edina, recalls

The Pinsent family in 1889, in the grounds at Selly Wick, at Sandy Hill, near Birmingham, where the family first lived after returning to England from Montevideo that year. Pinsent's parents, Adolphus Medoul Ross Pinsent (1852–1929) and Alice Mary (Nuttal) Pinsent (1854–1900), with their children (left to right): Frances Maude Pinsent (b. 1882), Cecil Ross Pinsent (b. 1884), Gerald (Gerry) Hume Saverie Pinsent (b. 1888), and Sidney Hume Pinsent (b. 1878).

the popular image of a North American Wild West homestead, and visits to the Lawries gave the children a taste of cowboy life. The wide-open spaces of the Uruguayan frontier would have been Pinsent's earliest experience of native landscape, a subject to which his senses were clearly attuned and which drew his attention in later life.

Cecil was five years old when the family returned to England; his mother had endured repeated bouts of ill health and England offered more sophisticated medical attention. They spent the first few months at Selly Wick, the home of Cecil's uncle, Richard Pinsent. The Pinsent family had a long heritage in the legal profession, and Richard was the head of a prosperous firm of Birmingham solicitors. The house was at Selly Hill, Edgbaston, near Birmingham, a city that in the latter half of the nineteenth cen-

The Estancia Edina, a ranch in Uruguay that belonged to family friends, where Pinsent spent part of his early childhood.

tury was an expanding industrial center surrounded by a rapidly developing urban sprawl. But the garden at Selly Wick retained its flavor of eighteenth-century exoticism. The garden was built in the remains of three worked-out clay pits, and its main feature was a steeply banked sunken pool. Dug into the bank were twin grottoes lit by stained-glass windows and linked by a mysterious tunnel. A sandstone pavilion built in the Gothic style overlooked the pool and grottoes. It was, as Cecil's cousin Sir Christopher Pinsent recalled, "a gloomy wonderland," but it was also a place of recreation, for picnic teas, winter skating parties, and so on. Fine specimen trees and graceful terraced lawns formed the approach to this picturesque folly, which was likely built in the early nineteenth century, the result of landscaping the clay pits to create pleasure gardens for the original late Georgian house. The garden couldn't be seen from the house, and a large part of its charm was the sense of isolated wonder and surprise it aroused.

In spring 1890 the Pinsent family moved to London, first to lodgings at Primrose Hill and then into their own house in Hampstead, a village that was gradually becoming a dormitory suburb of London. The house at 16 Maresfield Gardens, NW3, just above

Views of the garden at Selly Wick, the home of Pinsent's paternal uncle Sir Richard Pinsent, c. 1900. The grotto, sunken pool, and other elements of crumbling Gothic-style architecture were probably the remains of a Georgian folly that formed the grounds of an earlier house on the site. (Courtesy of Sir Christopher Pinsent.)

Finchley Road, is one of a row of substantial detached dwellings, at the time newly constructed. Pinsent's photographs of the house show that it had a large garden and pleasant views from the gently sloping site across the undeveloped fields and orchards north of London.

Pinsent's formal education began in 1893, when he was enrolled as a boarder at the Hartford House Preparatory School in Hartley Wintney, Hampshire. In 1897 he matriculated at Marlborough College, where his older brother, Sidney, and some of their cousins were also students. Marlborough was traditionally known as the school that built the British Empire by turning boys into lawyers and politicians. Pinsent's much younger half-brother, Basil, believed that Cecil did not enjoy his years at either school, yet photographs in Pinsent's archive, labeled "The Boys Gardens, Hartford House," suggest that this aspect of the school provided at least some degree of interest, as do photographs of the college grounds and surrounding landscape features, including pastoral views of the river Kennet. In photographing these tranquil views, Cecil may well have found not only a diverting hobby but some solace, too, at being consigned to a boarding school, for although, as Basil remarked, Cecil regarded his upbringing as "stuffy and strict," he, unlike some English schoolboys his age, found no pleasure in being sent away, but rather missed his siblings and family life. This was a sentiment he carried into mature life; according to Basil, family came first with Pinsent, and he was a loyal brother and, later, a devoted uncle, sending "amusing unbirthday gifts" to his nieces Jane and Chloe long after their birthdays had passed.

Pinsent was sixteen when his mother died in 1900. Basil Pinsent suggested that her years of poor health may have been, to some degree, a case of *"malades imaginaires;"* she was remembered by her children as a morose woman, stern and aloof, and a complete contrast to "Phil" Whitelaw, the bright, affable young woman who was at the time the family nanny, and whom Ross Pinsent married some three or four years later.

The turn of the century brought another change in Pinsent's life, as he left Marlborough at the end of the summer term, determined to study architecture. His father wanted him to pursue a career in law and follow the Pinsent family tradition by attending Cambridge University. But Cecil was adamant, and his father grudgingly relented. On March 15, 1901, the start of the spring

School portrait of Cecil Pinsent, age 11.

The boys' gardens at Hartford House Preparatory School, Hartley Wintney, Pinsent's first formal school.

term, Pinsent was elected as a student member of the Architectural Association. At this time students were articled (apprenticed) to an established architecture practice, doing menial tasks while studying with the Architectural Association school's tutors in the evenings. The tutors were also practicing architects, often quite eminent in the field. They would assign projects to their students and then evaluate and critique the final work in the open forum of the school's studio.

During his years at the Architectural Association school, Pinsent was articled to several prominent London architects. His first apprenticeship, arranged by his father, began in November 1901, when he went to work with the architect William Wallace, a family friend. Six months later, in May 1902, Wallace sent him to Burnham Market in Norfolk to measure "The Lodge," an aggregate of several centuries of architectural forms, typical of many old English manor-farmhouses, Pinsent completed his pupilage in 1903 and began work as a draftsman in Wallace's office. In 1905, on Wallace's recommendation, he was accepted as a student at the Royal Academy School of Architecture, and in November of that year he was employed as a draftsman at E. T. Hall's office in Bedford Square, where he worked on and off over the next three

Pinsent's colleagues in the drauftsmen's office at E. T. Hall.

The Lodge at Burnham Market, Norfolk. In July 1902, while articled to the London architect William Wallace, Pinsent was sent to measure this manor farmhouse as one of his first projects. The exercise of executing measured drawings was an essential part of architectural education, and remains so this day.

years. Pinsent studied at the Royal Academy School from January 1905 to September 1907.

At Hall's firm Pinsent enjoyed early exposure to evolving architectural styles that ranged from Tudor vernacular to neo-classical. Edwin Thomas Hall (1851–1923) was a prominent London architect and vice president of the Royal Institute of British Architects. His best-known work is the half-timbered façade of the Liberty department store in central London, but he was also the architect of the Old Library at Dulwich College and the Manchester Royal Infirmary, as well as several other hospitals. In 1907 he entered the design competition for the London County Hall at Westminster. His entry did not win the judges' favor, but Hall's section drawings and floor plans for the competition were published in *Building News* and the pages are preserved in Pinsent's archive, suggesting that he was involved in the preparation of the drawings.

During Pinsent's time there, the Royal Academy School was at the center of architectural radicalism, its tutors promulgating ideas of English renaissance formalism and rural vernacular as the source for a new language of English design and the Academy Library acquiring books that supported the new trends. Pinsent might well have read the library's copies of *Gothic Architecture, Old Cottages and Farmhouses in Kent and Sussex*, and *The Architecture of Renaissance Italy*. He no doubt attended Academy lectures by the highly respected architect and Academy tutor Thomas Graham Jackson, on such topics as "Architecture and the Craftsman" and "Reason in Architecture"— themes Jackson had been iterating for several years. When we come to look at Pinsent's mature work it seems to reflect the lesson in Jackson's preface to a collection of his lectures:

> The moral [this book] is intended to point is this. That the styles of the past, which we have been taught to take as our models, assumed the forms, under which we know them, not from arbitrary design or fancy, but as a consequence of rational and logical development from causes partly external and partly social . . . [That] our architecture will depend for its vitality upon its accommodation to the circumstances of the day. Consequently, that the mere blind following of ancient example in which most modern schools have thought to find safety will lead us no whither; that Archaeology is not Architecture; and that it is the spirit rather than the letter of the great styles of the past that will be of use to us.

Among the other influential architects of the day who were closely associated with the Royal Academy was Reginald Blomfield (1856–1942), author of *The Formal Garden in England*, who was first an Academy tutor and then, during Pinsent's last year at the school, Professor of Architecture. In 1904 Blomfield made a presentation to the Royal Institute of British Architects commenting on the new guidelines proposed by the Board of Architectural Education. In his closing paragraphs, Blomfield supported Jackson's views on architectural education, saying that he had "hit the nail on the head in one very important point: that is, that architecture, after all, was founded on reason. If it was not a matter based on the facts of existence and the practical handling of realities, it would have no serious touch with humanity at all."

The aim now for tutors was to rid their students of all shibboleths and conventions, to train them not to look upon any particular style or method as sacrosanct, and to encourage them to think for themselves, to use their materials freely and intelligently but with the full knowledge of what had been done in the past—a foundation they could not do without. History, not historicism, should inform the new architects' work, but observation was the key to understanding its application. Clough Williams-Ellis, one of England's more eclectic architects and Pinsent's contemporary, described in his autobiography the professional training young architects received at "the small but even then vigorous school" run by the Architectural Association. Williams-Ellis, too, had been set the task of making measured drawings, including, like Pinsent, ones of an old manor-farmhouse. Remembering the experience, he wrote that this work "is very properly held to be an important part of the young architect's training, and certainly when exercised on a subject of any distinction, this enforced intimacy with its every secret of proportion, detail, and construction, is a fine lesson in all the arts of building." That Pinsent understood and placed great value on this intimate scrutiny of the built environment is evident from the contents of the photograph albums documenting his travels around England on family holidays, and his several visits to Europe in the company of his father and brothers. During his student years Pinsent did not confine his study of buildings to school time, but carried his camera, pens, and measuring tools with him and put them to frequent and energetic use. His drawings during this time, too, record Gothic and vernacular architecture and ornament, as well as the regional landscapes he encountered, while the subjects he chose indicate an awareness of the interaction of buildings and the landscape in which they are sited.

Pinsent studied architecture near the end of a transitional period in the decorative arts known collectively as "The Battle of the Styles." For several decades before 1900, English architects had been arguing over what could legitimately be considered a

These drawings by Pinsent, dating from 1902–3, show that his observational and drawing skills were well developed by the time he began to study architecture. The Toll Gate, 1901, and Dicking House, 1903, both in Kent, England.

The cloister gardens at the twelfth-century early-Gothic Collégiale church, Neuchatel, Switzerland, photographed by Pinsent in early June 1901. The unadorned simplicity of the cloister and quadripartite garden left a lasting impression and were recalled in some of Pinsent's later works..

national style of architecture, and whether the constituent design elements of any such style could be said to be authentically English—not quite as empty as arguing over how many angels could sit on the head of a pin, but nearly. At the same time, there was an increasingly widely held belief that architects should be responsible not just for the design and ornament of a building but also for every facet of construction. Thus architectural education was due for an overhaul, since the acquisition of practical skills could no longer be ignored in favor of the development of aesthetic sensibilities. Students were to be trained in engineering skills as well as in drawing—to lay a drain as well as to delineate a volute. The subjects of several of Pinsent's drawings suggest that he followed the debates with some practical interest; he searched for English design language by studying Gothic structure and ornament as

An alpine church in Oberwald, photographed in June 1904 while Pinsent was traveling in Switzerland. He captioned the building above "avalanche plough" for the end of the building facing into the slope of the mountain; its purpose is to absorb the shock of an avalanche, which Pinsent also photographed (left), and to lessen the risk of the building's being swept down the mountain.

In March 1905 Pinsent explored the decorative application of Gothic and classical orders in these sketches for memorial plaques.

well as acquiring a working knowledge of classical orders. And his interest in all things mechanical was brought to bear on the workings of pulleys and automobile engines.

Pinsent was very much a product of the new approach to architectural training, and it changed the direction of his life. His final student project at the Royal Academy, a descriptive architectural history, with measured drawings and elevations, of Mansion House, the residence of the Lord Mayor of the City of London, a classical but unremarkable and much altered seventeenth-century building, is a marked contrast to his earliest project of sketching and measuring an early English rural vernacular building.

In August 1906 Pinsent won the Architectural Association's Banister Fletcher bursary, probably for the Mansion House project. The prize money of 25 guineas (roughly $2,500 or €2,000 in today's terms) likely financed his first trip to Italy. That extended tour, to which we will return shortly, lasted ten months, from October 1906 to July 1907, when Pinsent returned to England. In

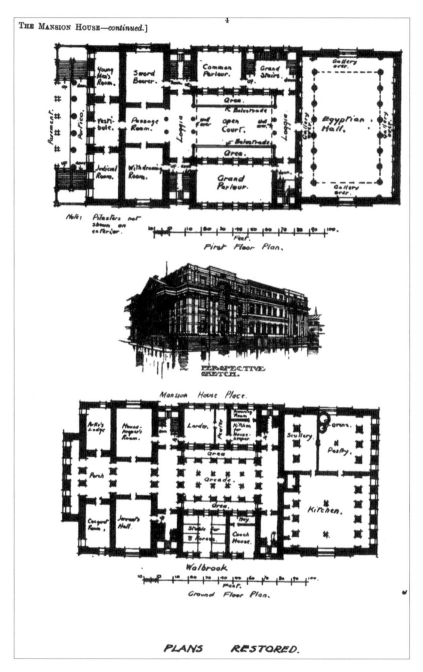

PLANS   RESTORED.

Pinsent's final student project for the Royal Academy was a set of measured drawings for Mansion House, London. He was awarded the Banister Fletcher bursary for this project, and likely used the money to fund his first trip to Italy.

the spring of 1907 he traveled around Tuscany with the Houghtons and his family, who had come to tour the villas of the northern lakes, Venice, and the Veneto. Then, in July, Pinsent returned to England and E. T. Hall's office while continuing his studies at the Architectural Association and Royal Academy schools. It is worth noting that during the time in Florence he had his first meeting with Bernard and Mary Berenson, and on his return to London met Geoffrey Scott for the first time, over lunch.

Pinsent was back in Italy in October 1907 "for work put in hand when on tour," although he did not specify the nature of this particular job. It was temporary, however, and in November he once again returned to London to work as a draftsman, dividing his time between the studio of E. W. Mountford (the architect of Sheffield Town Hall and many other major public buildings) and the offices of C. E. Mallows. Pinsent also passed his architecture exams and was subsequently accepted as an Associate of the Royal Institute of British Architects.

Pinsent's time with Mallows exposed him at close quarters to the history of garden design and planning. Charles Edward Mallows (1864–1915) designed a number of buildings in the Arts and Crafts style; he is best remembered today as the architect of Tirley Garth, a large country house in Cheshire, whose gardens he also designed. Mallows was a leading exponent of the "traditional," formal style of garden design as espoused by J. D. Sedding (1838–1891) and Reginald Blomfield. Garden design and landscape had also been included in the search for a "national style," and for some the formal gardens of the seventeenth century offered a model. Blomfield's book *The Formal Garden in England* (1892) advanced this idea, as did Sedding's *Garden-craft Old and New* (1891). Blomfield was an authority on Italian Renaissance architecture, and Sedding admired the Italian gardens of that period. "Of the garden of Italy," he wrote, "who shall dare to speak critically. Child of tradition: heir by unbroken descent, inheritor of the garden-craft of the whole civilised world . . . so frankly artistic, yet so subtly blending itself into the natural surroundings." Sedding prescribed the so-called old-fashioned formal garden, not only as the only truly English style of garden, but as the sort most fitting for the country houses being built by England's rising middle classes: "The sixteenth century, which saw the English garden formulated, was a time for grand enterprises; indeed, to this period is ascribed the making of England. These gardens, then, are the handiwork of the makers of England . . . They are relics of the men and women who made our land both fine and famous . . . ; [they represent] the patient craft of men versed in great affairs—big men, who thought and did big things."

Both Blomfield and Sedding admired the formal garden above the landscape park, and they also maintained that only architects were able to design gardens, since the garden was a natural extension of the house. This brought them into argument with William Robinson (1838–1935), an early follower of Ruskin, an advocate of the natural style of gardening and author of *The Wild Garden* (1870) and *The English Flower Garden* (1883). In 1892, in response to Sedding's book, Robinson published *Garden Design and Architects' Gardens*, in which he dismissed the formal garden as pure artifice and advocated an emotional response to nature. He also maintained that only those who knew about horticulture—gardeners—were capable of designing a garden. Thus did the Battle of the Styles spill over into landscape architecture.

Mallows was on the side of Blomfield and Sedding; his work was admired by the famous English garden designer and plantswoman Gertrude Jekyll (1843–1932), who nonetheless supported Robinson, and so came to shape early twentieth-century English garden design by combining formal plan with informal planting. Jekyll included examples of Mallows's drawings and plans for houses and gardens in her book *Gardens for Small Country Houses* (1911).

An understanding of Mallows's garden design aesthetic can be gained from the multipart article he contributed to *The Studio* titled "Architectural Gardening," prepared while Pinsent was working in his office. The first three parts were published between 1908 and 1909, just as Pinsent was establishing himself in Florence. Mallows's notes for this article include his observations on the relationship between a house and garden: that it is essential "to bring something of the character of the house into the garden

These drawings by Charles Edward Mallows of a house and cloister-like garden were used by Gertrude Jekyll in *Gardens for Small Country Houses*. Pinsent was employed by Mallows and would have been familiar with Mallows's knowledge and appreciation of garden design history.

in order to obtain unity of effect in both." "This point," he wrote, "cannot be too often repeated as therein lies one of the secrets of the success of garden design."

In 1905, just prior to Pinsent's joining his office, Mallows produced a small brochure describing his proposed designs for new municipal offices in Bournemouth. This project was described in *The Builder:* "[The] guiding principle was that its form should be determined by the outline of the site and the following out of this idea has led to the evolution of an exceedingly fine and architecturally effective form of plan which arises naturally out of the conditions of the site." Peter Davey, in his book *Art and Crafts Architecture: The Search for Earthly Paradise,* describes Mallows thus: "His work, as draftsman and architect, was always delicate and sensitive with deep respect for local tradition." Sensitivity to site and the architecture that develops from it was a precept that Pinsent seems to have absorbed in youth, realized as an architectural student, and then came to practice actively in Tuscany.

TWO

Italy: "How educating!"

Later in his life Pinsent wrote to his half-brother Basil, who was at the time considering his future course in life and had asked for advice: "Your dilemma reminds me of my own when 25 years old. It was a choice between plodding on in London, or plunging into what Pater rightly considered to be a wild speculation. As you know, I plunged, and from a point of view of living a full life have never regretted it . . . [W]ere I in your shoes I would go for the fuller, richer life . . . with its ferment of interests, political, intellectual and artistic, with its possibilities of contacts with all sorts of people and all the adventure of striking out for oneself."

In 1906 Pinsent's architecture studies were drawing to a close. He was working for one of England's top firms as a draftsman, and had received and begun work on his first commission, a small home for a single woman in a new development in Bournemouth. The client was Miss Jane Houghton, a Pinsent family friend through her brother Edmund Houghton and his wife, Mary. Around this time, too, Pinsent became engaged to Edmund's niece, Alice Houghton. He seemed set to establish himself in the traditional upper-middle-class role of a family man with a well-paid profession.

Pinsent's early prospects for success in England may have looked promising, but nevertheless his immediate future held lit-

This passport photo is dated October 1906, when Pinsent traveled to Italy with Mary and Edmund Houghton, staying at Signora Rodriguez Pensione on the via dei Seragli in Florence.

tle more than a position as a salaried draftsman or technician in an established architectural practice. London's noblesse and the newly wealthy of the booming industrial Midlands were already well served by a number of prominent architects. He determined, instead, to follow his instincts and the advice of Edmund Houghton and his wife, Mary, to explore the possibility of setting up a practice in Florence. Travel had broadened his horizons, and it might do just the same for his career. He began to plan a trip to Florence.

A generation older than Cecil Pinsent and close friends of the Pinsent family, Edmund and Mary Houghton were fringe members of the Souls, a group of English aesthetes that included the duchess of Rutland (Violet Manners), Lord Curzon, Lord and Lady Elcho (Hugo and Mary Charteris), and other Victorian beauties and gallants, who affected glib erudition in their discourse, loose stays in their clothing, and notions of chivalric love (brought down to earth with a smattering of carnal passion). Like their Souls friends, the Houghtons supported Pre-Raphaelite art, and they collected English antique furniture for

A panoramic view of Florence by Edmund Houghton. He was employed by Bernard Berenson to photograph paintings for Berenson's reference library.

their tiny cottage in deepest rural Sussex and Italian vintage pieces for their home in a medieval tower in Florence. Mary, more than Edmund, was an avid traveler, and they were in the vanguard of motor travel through Europe at a time when there were few paved roads. Mary Houghton's *In the Enemy's Country* (1915) describes a difficult car journey from Italy to England that she and Edmund undertook just as World War I was breaking out, trying to reach England from Florence before the borders closed. She makes a few references to Edmund from which a picture emerges of a thoughtful, gentle man with an amateur interest in astronomy and mathematics (which he shared with Pinsent). According to the landscape architect Sir Geoffrey Jellicoe, Houghton was "a true aesthete, unworldly, a perfect example of a dilettante, with no creative talent of his own, but capable of recognizing the creativity of others."

Edmund and Mary had lived in Italy for some years, first in Venice and then, from 1900, in Florence, in a medieval tower at 32 via dei Bardi, where Edmund was able to keep a telescope on the roof. In urging Pinsent to travel to Italy, the Houghtons no doubt encouraged him to believe that he could eventually become a large fish in a small pond. The Houghtons knew many of the more influential and wealthy expatriates in Florence, and so were able to introduce Pinsent to potential clients who were constructing new villas and gardens or renovating old properties in the

Houghton's photographs of the exterior and interior of the couple's home, a tower on the via dei Bardi. Note the vintage furnishings and utensils; the Houghtons dealt in antiques and fine art. Mary Houghton can be seen standing in the doorway.

hillside towns of Fiesole and Settignano to the east of the city. They would, the Houghtons explained, find it far easier to deal with an English-trained and English-speaking architect than with the native craftsmen and workers, who were routinely regarded with suspicion and not a little disdain.

The Houghtons convinced Pinsent to join them on a lengthy tour of Tuscany, and the group set off in the autumn of 1906, with plans to stay at least until the summer of 1907. With a nod to Pinsent's mechanical ability, the Houghtons made a pretense of employing him as their driver, but in fact Edmund seems to have had Pinsent's development as an architect uppermost in mind. Basil Pinsent related his telling of the story: "[Edmund would] stop his car, and, Cecil said, 'He told me to wander off while he fixed the [car].' So I wandered off and I found this magnificent ruin, shrines and everything.' And he said to Edmund, 'Well, have you seen this,' and Edmund said, 'Why do you think

Cecil Pinsent playing the "*Bon homme*," as he captioned this photograph, and pretending to fix the touring car, a De Dion, in April 1907. Pinsent's father and his brother Gerry were visiting him that spring, and the group toured Pisa, Venice, Padua, and Verona (where Pinsent photographed the cloister of the church of S. Zeno), as well as visiting Florence.

Mary and Edmund Houghton on either side of Pinsent, picnicking by the Frigido, December 1906. On Christmas Day the friends were at Massa Carrara, the famed Marble Mountains, where Pinsent took time to sketch the rock formations.

I stopped the car? If you hadn't seen it or noticed it, as far as an architect is concerned, I wouldn't have thought much of you.' It was a nasty little test." Pinsent also recalled Edmund's "fetching me off the Palazzo Nonfinito, which in my innocence I was measuring, and telling me to go and measure the Pazzi Chapel first and come back to the Nonfinito if I felt like it after. I never did."

Pinsent's photograph albums document the group's itinerary from Siena to Volterra, San Gimignano, and Venice, as well as the environs of Fiesole. During this trip he was exposed to an enormous variety of architectural periods and styles, ornamentation, and landscape that would have brought to life the concepts and values he absorbed as a student. He made pencil drawings of Italian churches, line drawings of landscapes and buildings, and a more finished and elaborate measured drawing of a Florentine palace. Visits to the walled hilltop towns of Tuscany provided examples of organically integrated architecture and landscape, while Siena's vividly colored cathedral, with its stratified layers of marble in tints of green, black, and cream that change the building's appearance with every shift in the sun's angle, illustrated how materials and light interact to create the most vivid decoration. The exoticism of Venice, with its quasi-oriental ornamentation, surely reminded the young architect of Ruskin's *Stones of Venice* and the belief of an earlier genera-

San Frediano in Cestello, in the Oltrarno section of Florence. Pinsent's drawing, made in November 1906, emphasizes the cupola and notes the architect, Antonio Maria Ferri, and the date, 1680.

Santa Maria del Carmine (now known as San Niccolò del Carmine), Siena. Pinsent drew the campanile in December 1906.

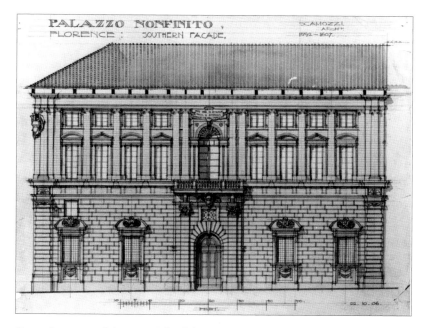

Pinsent's measured drawing of the Palazzo Nonfinito, which bears a passing resemblance to London's Mansion House, which he also drew as his final student project. Pinsent completed this drawing despite Edmund Houghton's advice that he focus his attention instead on the nearby Pazzi Chapel, one of the architectural gems of the Florentine Renaissance, by Filippo Brunelleschi. Pinsent obliged, and it was one of the earliest experiences that shaped his evolving comprehension of the importance of architectural space.

tion of architects that the practice of architecture was truly the art of decoration, a belief that Pinsent's generation was set to dismantle.

•

The Houghtons soon introduced their protégé to possible clients. Edmund had taken up photography, which, according to Bernard Berenson's longtime secretary, "he developed into a real art," becoming a proficient photographer of landscape, architecture, and fine art. Bernard and Mary Berenson employed him to record paintings for the reference library they were establishing at the dilapidated coaching inn they had begun to renovate into a gracious and comfortable villa. Called Villa I Tatti, it is located in the hillside town of Settignano, just outside Florence. The Houghtons introduced Pinsent to the Berensons when they stayed as guests at I Tatti, a few weeks after New Year's Day 1907.

The BBs, as the couple was collectively known, were among the most influential members of the expatriate community in Florence, social refugees whose volatile relationship, wide and influential circle of friends in Italy, England, and America, and tireless self-promotion had a direct bearing on Pinsent's professional and personal life. As they were the youthful Pinsent's first contacts with the diverse and worldly society of Edwardian Florence, it is important to understand something of who these people were and how they came to be the gravitational center of the expatriate community.

Mary Berenson was a more substantial and significant figure than history has allowed. She was the daughter of Hannah and Robert Pearsall Smith, a prominent family of Philadelphia Quakers who migrated to England, where they became part of the literary and artistic society known as the Arts and Crafts movement. The Pearsall Smiths were social reformers; Robert was regarded as a brilliant preacher who advanced the controversial Wesleyan doctrine known as "entire sanctification." But he came to the controversial belief that free expression of physical love was the route to divine love, and he eventually had to return to America in disgrace. He was utterly cast down, and soon abandoned his faith entirely.

Hannah Pearsall Smith was of entirely different composition. While not relishing the sexual side of married life, she nonetheless gave birth to seven children, only three of whom survived to adulthood: Mary, the eldest (1864–1945), a son, Logan (1865–1946), and another daughter, Alys (1868–1951). Hannah was a prototype feminist, and she cherished her daughters more than her son; her ambition for them and her passion to provide them with the very best education to ensure that they could stand as intellectual equals with men was extraordinary for her time. Mary studied at Smith College and then philosophy at the newly established Harvard Annex (later Radcliffe College). The poet Walt Whitman, a family friend, nicknamed Mary his "Bright Particular Star."

In 1885, when she was twenty-one years old, Mary Pearsall Smith married Frank Costelloe, a London barrister with political aspirations who came from a landed but impoverished Anglo-Irish family. To begin with, Mary made the furtherance of his political career her main task in life, as well as being the perfectly domesticated wife and mother—much to the despair of her mother, who was afraid that Frank would prove to be the thing she loathed most, "an authoritarian husband." But it was not long before Mary's efforts to raise Frank's political profile began to raise her own instead, and she was soon being urged to campaign in her own name for women's rights, temperance, and moral reform. But as Mary's light began to shine more brightly her husband's began to dim, and it was not long before Mary realized that he was determined to stifle her aspirations and by emotional blackmail force her back into her "womanly role." Her mother had been right.

The first of the Costelloes' two children, Rachel, affectionately known as Ray, was born in June 1887, soon after Mary was pregnant again with a second daughter, Karin, born in March 1889. Mary felt the noose tightening; her husband's career path took another downward spin and she sank into a deep depression. In February 1889 she wrote to her mother complaining that she was simply being dragged along in Frank's wake and had no separate life of her own in which she felt she could become successful. In her private journal on December 9, 1889, she lectured herself: "Here is the life to be lived . . . and I must try to live it . . . Therefore, woman, sink thyself and thy needs and empty hopes. They cannot be fulfilled. Join the army of those who exist to fill up the gaps in the interesting lives of others, and learn, as most women learn, to consider it enough interest for thee." But her good intentions were not enough to satisfy her need to realize her own ambitions, which chiefly consisted of a burning desire to live a stimulating intellectual life, pursuing her political and creative interests on an equal footing with any male within her circle.

Bernhard (he dropped the "h" later in life) Berenson was a Jewish émigré from Lithuania; he was ten years old when he and his younger sister, Bessie, arrived in Boston in 1875 with their parents. His father became an itinerant peddler working a route between Massachusetts and Maine; his mother took in lodgers. A brilliant student, he attended the Boston Latin School and Harvard. Upon graduation he applied for, but failed to win, a traveling fellowship to study art and culture in Europe. His single-minded ambition brought him the support of several wealthy patrons, including the well-known art collector Isabella Stewart Gardner. Berenson arrived in Italy in 1887 and soon embarked on a serious study of Italian painting, guided by the scholar Giovanni Morelli (1816–1891), who had developed a method of studying paintings through what he termed "comparative analysis." Berenson was an adept and quickly became Mrs. Gardner's adviser on Italian Renaissance art and, at a time when other wealthy collectors were focused on English and French art, helped her build a formidable collection of Italian art, which was eventually housed at Fenway Court in Boston, now the Isabella Stewart Gardner Museum.

In the summer of 1890 Mary Costelloe and Bernard Berenson met for only the second time, yet in a matter of months (encouraged by Mary's college friend Gertrude Hitz Burton, who was one of Berenson's supporters) the two became lovers. Mary sailed to Italy with Berenson in August 1891, ostensibly for a year's work studying the history of Italian art under his tutelage. Frank Costelloe had agreed to this arrangement, hoping it would provide the stimulus she needed and so mend their shaky marriage; he even allowed the children to go to Florence, where Mary and Bernard had settled in adjacent apartments, for a six-month visit. Hannah Smith also came to visit, attempting to understand her daughter's—and Bernard's—intentions.

Two years later Mary asked her husband for a divorce, but Costelloe, who was a Roman Catholic, refused. Instead he agreed to a formal separation, but on condition that Mary relinquish her parental rights. Though desolated by the loss of her children, Mary cast her lot with Berenson. She was not troubled by her ostracism from English society, because she felt that in Italy she had found the sort of spiritual and intellectual freedom for which she had been searching.

Mary was attracted to Berenson by his urbanity and intellectual sophistication. She was intrigued by the "scientific" method of criticism and attribution he had developed, and she saw an opportunity to establish a relationship based on mutual intellectual respect and support, with herself in the role of Berenson's student and amanuensis, helping to make him the greatest in his field. She saw herself as his partner in rewriting the history of Italian art according to his methods of attribution, in the silent hope that she, too, would become recognized as a notable art historian.

The irregular situation of their life in Florence hardly mattered to the Anglo-American community, many of whom were themselves living or traveling extensively abroad due to the unusual circumstances of their own lives. Among their circle of friends the Berensons counted the then influential novelist and essayist Vernon Lee (Violet Paget) and her intimate companion, Kit Anstruther-Thomson; the philosopher and psychologist William James and his brother Henry; English writers Katherine Bradley and her niece, Edith Cooper, who published highly fashionable "Jacobean" verse dramas and lyric poetry under the joint pen name Michael Field, in which they professed their lesbian love affair. The Irish poet and playwright Oscar Wilde was a particular friend of Mary's, as was Edith Wharton.

Mary seems to have inherited her father's idea that free love was the way to spiritual enlightenment, and in the spring of 1895 she began an affair with a young sculptor, Hermann Obrist, while Bernard was in the United States building a clientele for his attribution business and confirming his growing reputation as one of the foremost art critics of the day. She wrote to tell Bernard of her undying love at the same time as she wrote to Obrist that she held their relationship to be uniquely natural and without guile.

Mary's self-described desire was always to be honest, true to self, open, and frank, to hide nothing and to ask nothing, but she rarely achieved these worthy goals. She saw herself as able to inspire her lovers and protégés to great things through her own self-sacrificing devotion, but she was repeatedly disappointed and cast down, always ending where she had left off with Frank—filling up the gaps in the interesting lives of others. And it was not too long before Bernard began finding other women to fill up the gaps in his own life—but only after he and Mary sat down together and read through her passionate correspondence with Obrist, to analyze the "true nature" of the affair. It is difficult to know how much Mary minded her open relationship with Berenson, but ultimately she did not have the protective, egotistical shell possessed by her husband, and even though she professed to be delighted when he found an attractive and intellectually suitable woman, her sense of her own worth took a knock.

Frank Costelloe died in 1899; Mary was at his deathbed and there was a reconciliation. But in his will Frank gave the care and control of their daughters to guardians, and although Mary fought against this provision—she had believed that Frank's death would give her back her children—the best she was able to achieve was that the girls would be allowed to live with her mother, Hannah, in London. His death did allow Mary and Bernard to marry, which they did in Florence on December 29, 1900. It seems that Bernard was not the most compliant groom; the marriage was motivated more by Mary's need to establish a regular household for the sake of her children, whose occasional presence Berenson tolerated. He felt that his interests, comfort, and well-being should be the

Bernard and Mary Berenson in the garden at I Tatti, May 1922.

central focus of his partner's life, as well as the concern of anyone else who crossed his path.

The civil ceremony in the town hall of Fiesole was followed by a Catholic ceremony in the tiny chapel attached to the villa that Berenson set about transforming into a temple to art and a palace of refined comfort and elegance, to provide the perfect setting in which he could hold court. His reputation as a connoisseur and critic was now international; he was the resident expert of Joseph Duveen's renowned gallery in Paris, whose clients included the tycoons and oil barons of America as well as European nobility and art museums around the world. Duveen paid Berenson an annual retainer as well as a percentage commission on any sales made through Berenson's agency. Duveen once remarked, "Berenson may know what's authentic, but only I know what will sell." And there lay the difference in their motivations: Berenson was interested only in aesthetic values, while Duveen cared only for what would sell. Their partnership endured for thirty years, unraveling only when Berenson refused to back up Duveen's attribution of a painting to close a lucrative sale.

For nearly fifty years, Mary and Bernard Berenson lived at I Tatti in a state of mutual despair, each lamenting the other's failings—with Berenson blaming the turmoil in his life on his wife's lapses of judgment or meddling in the affairs of others, while she tried to maintain her emotional balance in the face of her egotistical husband's serial philandering and cruel temper tantrums. The creation of the Villa I Tatti and the magnificent gardens that surround it were often the cause of their more fraught moments together, but the villa would become Pinsent's first major Italian commission, and the one that established his position as the architect of choice in Florence. That could not have been foretold at the outset, however. After their first meeting, at I Tatti on January 21, 1907, Mary Berenson wrote to her mother, "We have had a young architect named Pinsent, the Houghtons' 'adopted son,' staying here. He seems nice but not very exciting . . . we talked and talked and the boy listened in a kind of daze. At the end he said, 'How educating!' but I wonder if he could have meant it."

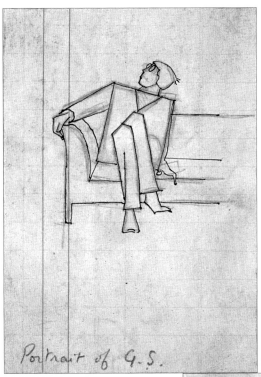

Portrait of G. S.

Two cartoons, one of Geoffrey Scott above, all brittle sharp edges, and the other of Mary Berenson, right, hand raised to stifle a yawn . . . of ennui?

M. B.

1912

THREE

Circles of Influence

Returning to England in July 1907 at the end of his trip to Italy, Pinsent prepared for a new life ripe with new potential: he would complete work on Jane Houghton's house in Bournemouth, leave his position at William Wallace's firm, and set his affairs in order for a speedy return to Italy, where he'd prepare a home for his soon-to-be wife, Alice Houghton, and establish his own architecture practice. To this end, he had already signed up one client—Charles Loeser, one of Berenson's friends from Harvard, who was remodeling a villa in Fiesole—and the Houghtons were urging Mary Berenson to dispense with their Italian architect in favor of the young Englishman. Mary Berenson would not only give him the break he needed to establish this new practice; she was about to introduce him to his future business partner, Geoffrey Scott.

Pinsent was a little more than a month older than Scott, who was born on June 11, 1884. Though they shared similar socio-economic backgrounds, there were significant dissimilarities that set them quite apart from each other and might have suggested that as business partners they were ill-matched. Like Pinsent's father, Scott's was a successful businessman, the proprietor of a linoleum manufacturing company. Scott was born in Hampstead, an upper-middle-class enclave on the northern fringe of London, and he was still living there six years later when Pinsent and his family moved to Hampstead. As was common for young men of their class, both were sent to highly respected public schools, Pinsent to Marlborough and Scott to Rugby. But at this point their lives diverge; Pinsent moved into architecture training in 1900, while Scott decided to leave Rugby after completing only the first of two years in the sixth or highest form, because he had been accepted at New College, Oxford, for the autumn term of 1902. Scott was a capable enough student, but like so many sheltered young people whose first taste of freedom comes with college, he would probably have achieved more and done better at his exams had he spent less time socializing and more time studying. At the end of 1905, as Pinsent was beginning his apprenticeship at Wallace's architectural firm, Scott was beginning his final year at Oxford with little clear indication of what he would do after graduation. It seemed that aimless ambition was to be his lot in life.

In spring 1906, while Pinsent was completing his studies and making preparations to tour Italy with the Houghtons, Scott and a Cambridge classmate, John Maynard Keynes, were looking forward to making their own excursion to Tuscany as traveling companions for Mary Berenson's daughters, Ray and Karin, on a motor tour of Italy. This trip, during March and most of April, would be Scott's first visit to the continent, and his first encounter with the Berensons. Mary immediately developed a crush on Scott, and she convinced Berenson that he would make an ideal personal assistant and secretary once his degree was completed. Scott's frailties and unformed talent brought out her nurturing instincts, and she determined to help him become the great writer she was sure he could be, if only he "could enjoy better health" and "be less susceptible to depressions and moods." One aspect of Scott's nature, however, caused her particular concern: in common with a number of his college contemporaries, Scott developed unrequited, distant passions for beautiful young boys. As she became infatuated with him, this provided her with an opportunity, not wholly altruistic, to express concern and offer the advice that "such affections might well be beautiful and inspiring in youth but become dotty and disgusting" if pursued into middle age; she urged him to pay more attention to his studies lest he fail to pass his exams. Scott replied that he recognized this character in several university dons, and for himself hoped that he would eventually grow out of it.

Nevertheless, he continued to neglect his studies and so received only a second-class degree. A better degree would have made diplomatic service or a fellowship for postgraduate study possible, and most importantly for Scott, assured him a respectable income, independent of the small annual allowance he received from his father. Teaching in a public school or a clerkship in the civil service might have offered him a career, but he regarded these prospects as beneath his intellect. Mary Berenson offered to help find him a post at an American university, an employment that would have been more acceptable to his self-esteem, but ultimately nothing was deemed suitable, while Scott nursed his dream of remaining an independent scholar supported by a literary career, an aspiration fostered by his winning, during his final term, the respected Chancellor's English Essay Prize presented in 1908. The contest, one of many sponsored by the university, was for an essay on a set topic; in Scott's year it was English architecture, and his essay was titled "The National Character of English Architecture," a topic that Pinsent was also engaging with in his architectural education. It is here that Pinsent's and Scott's paths begin to intersect, one young man building a future by applying his practical talents, the other his intellectual skills.

In the summer of 1907, while Pinsent was winding up his affairs in London in advance of returning to Florence to begin work, Scott came back to I Tatti to spend time with Mary Berenson. He, too, was eager to embark on a career that might bring prestige as well as profit, and during that visit she convinced him that architecture would suit his purpose while allowing him the opportunity to develop his interest in writing on art and aesthetics. She was laying the groundwork for her scheme to keep Scott close.

Mary and Scott returned to England for family visits, and over lunch on August 13 she introduced him to Pinsent. As she described the meeting in her diary entry for that day, Pinsent had treated architecture "as a very irrelevant and secondary sort of matter," while all Scott had wanted to know was "how many holidays there were." And so it seems the pattern was set for the partnership that was yet to come, as Scott decided that becoming an architect was not a bad idea and offered his best course of action. It held the promise of a comfortable income and plenty of time to write. He enrolled in the Architectural Association School of Architecture, the same school Pinsent had attended seven years earlier; his name, however, appears on the student list for only the first term of the academic year beginning in September 1907. It wasn't long before he found the discipline of applied study and measured drawing boring, writing to Mary, "I feel about as conscious as an oyster," and then a month later, "I get up in the morning, go to school, or perhaps don't."

Scott soon abandoned this one and only attempt at gaining a formal training in architecture, and in March 1908 once again started looking for work. He was rejected for a civil service position but eventually, on the recommendation of Mary Berenson, was accepted as a traveling companion for the son of one of the Berensons' friends and fellow expatriates, the American banker Henry Cannon, on the young man's "Grand Tour" through France and Italy. Scott went out to Italy in early April, but this endeavor was cut short when, on May 27, he returned to England following the death of his father. For the remaining seven months of 1908 Scott stayed with his family while trying to find work in the civil service, but in the end he remained unemployed.

Mary Berenson's devotion to the cause of Scott's future enraged Berenson, who expected her to focus entirely on his needs and comfort. Writing to Mary before Scott's arrival in 1908, Berenson scolded, "I shall be delighted to see Scott but I do expect you to help me with my work just as if he were not here. If you do not I shall be extremely put out. Then remember I do not envy the smashing up of the pleasant illusion that here at least in our house I am first in your heart." But now, after a year of bickering and fuming, a contrite Mary declared to Berenson that her interest in Scott was waning. "[Scott] is perhaps a little on my nerves for his limpness," she wrote a few weeks later, adding that "the only inexhaustible topic is the depressing one of his future, which we have discussed *ad nauseam* . . . I want to be kind to him in so far as I can without interfering in thy comfort or the general things we want to do."

During this time the Berensons had completed the purchase of I Tatti and had begun work to convert it into an elegant villa with all the modern conveniences of indoor plumbing and electricity. The Berensons had been in the United States when the renovations began; when they returned to Florence they found that little progress had been made, and what had been achieved was badly done and not acceptable to Berenson's exacting standards. So it was that in 1909, nearly eighteen months after he had been the Berensons' post–New Year's house guest in company with the Houghtons, they engaged Pinsent as their architect. According to the rare book dealer Allen Thomas, who knew Pinsent in his old age, Pinsent recalled that he was hired first as an intermediary, then as the architect in charge.

Given Mary Berenson's obvious attachment to Scott, and his acknowledgment that architecture offered an acceptable career path, it's easy enough to understand why he accepted her idea of becoming Pinsent's business partner. Why Pinsent accepted is not so clear, but a letter he wrote to Mary in 1911 suggests that he recognized the value of working with someone who possessed qualities that he did not: "Ours was a partnership of opposites, complementary gifts . . . Scott is intellectual, literary and brilliant, with the gift of words, and I practical, inventive, with aptitude for things visible to the eye, but dumb."

The partnership did not, it must be made clear, get off to a running start. Arriving in Florence in April 1909 to begin work, Scott immediately fell ill, first with lumbago and other rheumatic pains, then an attack of boils, which left him depressed and unable to participate in any kind of architectural work. As Mary Berenson described it, "He gets up about noon and has an Italian lesson, browses with Greek and Italian books in a chaise-longue all day . . . and creeps to bed quite tired at 10–10:30."

With Pinsent actively engaged in the I Tatti project and drumming up other clients and smaller jobs, Scott's attention was diverted to another job, also arranged by Mary Berenson, assisting the American interior designer Ogden Codman (co-author

View of I Tatti, May 1901, showing the newly planted cypress avenue and the library wing.

The interior of the library at I Tatti, photographed in 1910, designed by Pinsent.

Mary Berenson's desk and cabinets, furnished by Scott and designed by Pinsent. October 1910.

with Edith Wharton of *The Decoration of Houses*), in arranging a catalogue raisonné of French chateaux. In early July Scott moved to the Codmans' chateau near Beauvais; unfortunately, however, Codman's materials turned out to be little more than a large collection of picture postcards and any serious scholarly work seemingly the last thing intended. Scott stayed on in France until September 1909, when he returned to his family in England. He had notions of expanding his prize-winning Chancellor's Essay into a larger work. And he still had the idea of continuing his partnership with Pinsent, living in the I Tatti *villino*, or worker's cottage, while helping with the renovations. In March 1910 he was back in Florence, but immediately took off on a buying trip around Europe to help furnish I Tatti. From May to September he toured Europe with a friend, returning to Florence to help Mary decorate; she describes his "hanging pictures" in the rooms at I Tatti. Thus it is certainly fair to question just how active Scott was in Pinsent's practice, since during 1909, the first year of their partnership, he was in Florence for all of two months, and in 1910 for possibly six months.

•

In early spring 1911 Scott and Pinsent took an apartment at 5 via delle Terme; Pinsent had been living at 3 via delle Terme while Scott had occupied the *villino* at I Tatti. Pinsent achieved much at I Tatti during this time. A six-page letter from him to Mary Berenson in August 1911 recounts progress on the structural alterations, and in March he had described the garden as "growing merrily." In a letter to her family in October, Mary Berenson included a sketch of the formal terrace garden.

Another major development in Pinsent's life came in 1911 with the commission to design and build Le Balze, a villa and garden in Fiesole, for Charles Augustus Strong, an American expatriate resident in Florence who was a patron of one of Berenson's Harvard friends, the philosopher George Santayana. Up until this

Geoffrey Scott taking in the scene, perched on the fountain in the center of the Piazza Navona, Rome, June 1912.

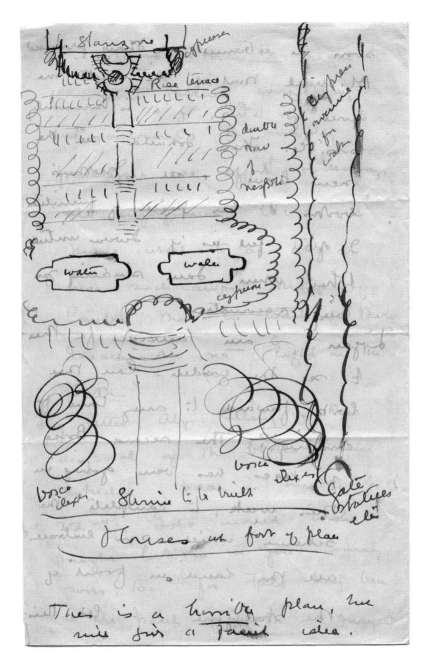

In a letter dated August 1911 to her brother Logan Pearsall Smith, Mary included a rough sketch of the formal garden taking shape at I Tatti and asked for his candid opinion. Mary was having doubts about the scheme and her young architect. (Courtesy of the Lilly Library, Indiana University, Bloomington, Indiana.)

time Pinsent's commissions in Italy had been for renovations, garden designs, and additions, but this was his first for a completely new structure and landscape. Talks began in 1911; the proposed site and its plan fell through in 1912, but work on the villa in its present site began in 1913,

As Pinsent's career matured, so did Scott's ambition to become an author of note; during 1912–13, while his partner was busy with the Le Balze project and continuing work at I Tatti, Scott concentrated on writing *The Architecture of Humanism*, while also traveling around Europe and helping Pinsent at Le Balze, where he seems to have been most involved in setting the style of the interior decoration and acquiring furnishings. Evidently Pinsent was not satisfied with the partnership, however, as he complained to Mary Berenson that Scott was not doing his share of the work. Writing to her daughter Karin, Mary outlined the problem: "Cecil works very hard, and Geoffrey practically doesn't work at all." Despite the numerous distractions that kept Scott from his work, he completed *The Architecture of Humanism* and it was published in June 1914. Some regarded it as revolutionary, while others observed that it was "demolishing old aesthetic theories rather than creating new ones." But because the publication coincided with the start of World War I, the book received little critical notice.

The outbreak of war affected Pinsent, too, and according to his client records his practice was kept ticking over by small-scale projects like the one in 1915, which came from Lady Sybil Cutting (formerly Lady Sybil Cuffe, second of the 5th Earl of Desart's two children; married to American banker William Bayard Cutting, as a widow she lived at Villa Medici with their only child, Iris Origo). Pinsent was to lay out the lower terrace garden at the historic Villa Medici, Fiesole, where in 1911 he had executed "alterations, sanitation [and] heating." And making "sponge-stone mosaics at BB's." (This work was one of Pinsent's trademarks; it is made from chunks of spongelike volcanic rock. Known as *spugna*, it is typical in the decoration of Renaissance garden features such as grottoes and retaining walls.)

In 1915, too, he enlisted; he was stationed in Verona and

remained there until the armistice. His chief duty was driving a British Red Cross ambulance that carried a portable X-ray machine which he learned to operate; the machine and truck had been funded in part by donations from his Florentine clients, including C. A. Strong and Henry Cannon. Pinsent's military service had been orchestrated by Mary Berenson, who, understanding the young man's commitment to "doing his part," was determined to find him a duty that would satisfy his need to be involved while at the same time keep him relatively safe. (Pinsent was wounded during his service, but the injury was minor.) Tending an X-ray machine engaged Pinsent's mechanical mind as well as permitting him to be useful. He was also among the soldiers who volunteered for rescue duty when a devastating earthquake rocked the south-central city of Avezzano, obliterating the town and killing 96 percent of its population, some 30,000 people. The Florentine expatriates rallied to support him, sending food parcels and clothing for the survivors and, incredibly, a case of champagne and assorted other delicacies for Pinsent's sustenance.

In January 1915, as this photograph is dated, Pinsent was at Avezzano as part of the Florentine rescue squad for the relief of the earthquake-stricken city.

Pinsent obtained only one further commission during the war years; in 1916 Princess Mary Thurn und Taxis asked him to design a "small rococo chapel" at Castle Duino in Gorizia, but by Pinsent's account this was never executed. Scott, because of his frail health, could not realistically enlist, although he frequently complained at not being able to do his bit. He remained in Florence working at I Tatti and, as his biographer writes, "brooding through much of 1915 and 1916 as to what to do with his life." This question was temporarily answered in autumn 1916 when, through Berenson's connections, he was offered a position in Rome as an assistant to the British ambassador's wife, helping with her charity work.

Pinsent and Scott's architectural partnership effectively ended with the war, although the two would remain friends. A few months after the armistice, Pinsent wrote to a close friend about his feelings, revealing that following his release from the Red Cross he was looking forward to returning to "beloved Via delle Terme, to pick up the strings of work again—my own work this time." Whether he was referring to leaving the Red Cross or to no longer being connected to Scott and the Berensons, and thus being able to establish his own independent practice, it's hard to say. It is, however, a clear expression of a desire to resume the work that throughout his life he regarded as his true vocation.

Despite his eagerness to pick up the threads of work, Pinsent would find it difficult to restart his architectural practice. There is no need to recount here the devastation the conflict wrought on an entire generation, and how it altered the shape of society. During the war many of his clients suffered catastrophic personal losses, and more than a few found themselves financially strained. Most were more concerned with rebuilding their lives than constructing elegant homes. Times were slow and the future remained uncertain.

•

Since the end of his engagement to Alice Houghton (for reasons unknown, although it may have been caused by the self-avowed fickleness of his nature when it came to intimate attachments),

Pinsent had enjoyed a number of liaisons with beautiful women, and his letters to Mary Berenson track the ups and downs of these relationships. Among the most memorable, apparently, was the fling he enjoyed in 1913 with Eve Fairfax, a destitute society beauty who was living off the kindness of friends in high places. She was then forty-two years old to his twenty-nine, and renowned as the model for a bust by Rodin (sometimes also called *La Nature*, versions of which exist in museums around the world), which had been commissioned in 1901 as a wedding gift by her fiancé, Ernest Beckett. Beckett ultimately deserted Eve, either because she hadn't a fortune to compensate for his loss of one, or because of the intimate relationship that she developed with Rodin. Pinsent enthusiastically described his passionate interludes to Mary as "the two most delicious nights I have ever spent." He goes on to describe almost cartoonish visions of a lithe figure flitting in and out of the sheer white curtains fluttering in the moonlit breeze. It was pure sexual pleasure for them both, and commitments did not enter into it.

Pinsent also developed a crush on the Hon. Irene Constance Lawley. Born in May 1889, Irene was Sybil Cutting's first cousin (their mothers were sisters), and she was also a friend

Among Pinsent's glamorous paramours during his early days in Florence was the sophisticated, older, and rather notorious English beauty Eve Fairfax, portrayed in this bust by Auguste Rodin. In 1913 Pinsent and Eve enjoyed an affair, during which he recalled spending some of the "most delicious nights" he had ever experienced.

In a photograph dated February 1913, the vivacious Irene Lawley, Sybil Cutting's cousin, skated into Pinsent's life. She was one of his earliest flirtations after ending his engagement to Alice Houghton. But it never went further, and the two remained firm friends all their lives.

of Eve Fairfax. Pinsent was immediately drawn to the young woman's infectious joie de vivre, as is evident from the cartoons and costumes he designed for her various entertainments; her love of theater inspired Pinsent to design and build a miniature theater, complete with scene changes and lighting. Pinsent's letters to Lawley span nearly twenty-five years, beginning with a clever little note penned in December 1912, the text in a tiny square of words centered on each sheet of note paper, the better, he quips, to have plenty of hyphens. As the years pass the tone alters from the flirtatious to friendly fondness, but through the letters can be traced Pinsent's penchant for mechanical invention, including a tool made of wood and wire, materials he amusingly dubs "my old friends," to help with the accuracy and rapidity of outdoor landscape sketching. He tells Irene that he prepared special sketchbooks from some sheets of seventeenth-century ledger paper he'd come across, calculated exactly how many sketches they would accommodate, and had already made a start with scenes from the quarries at Maiano. Geoffrey Scott, hearing this, teased Pinsent, saying that he would probably execute ten or twelve sketches before getting tired of the whole project because, Pinsent explained, "He's always said that I

Old Fiesole, in an early nineteenth-century engraving showing the rural hillside town and the Villa Medici's prominent position, just below the brow of the hill.

prefer means to ends, but I've always answered that what *he* calls means *are* ends." He goes on to admit that he probably would "let it all drop" if the sketches didn't meet his own expectations. Like so many artists, Pinsent was his own worst critic.

Scott's teasing observations may have been rooted in the work Pinsent was carrying out at the Villa Medici in 1921, designing a Chinese library. Having done the garden restoration, he now confronted making interior alterations to one of the most exceptional villas in Florence. His clients were Scott and his new wife, Sybil Cutting, whom he had married in 1918. A few years later, writing to Irene, Pinsent described the tension he experienced, and it says much about his work habits and creative process. "[I had] set myself to do an ambitious task, so ambitious that I was terrified by it, and *could not* get started," he wrote, adding that once he finally did commence sketching a scheme, the least little distraction served to "break the thread and everything would get held up." Ultimately he shut himself away so that the sketches could not be seen in their intermediate stages. The final result was a complete success, but looking back on it, Pinsent said, it seemed "like a nightmare."

Just two years later Scott, having seemed to have finally found a path, began to wander again in an emotional and creative fog. In 1923 he began a disastrous affair with the English literary figure Vita Sackville-West, later known as the creator of the renowned

Contemporary views of Villa Medici, Fiesole: The approach to the villa, and the terrace garden renovated by Pinsent for Sybil Cutting. (Ethne Clark)

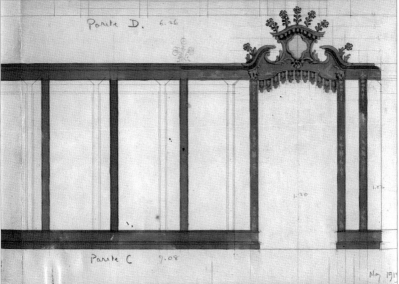

In addition to restoring the terrace garden below the loggia, Pinsent was employed by Scott and his new wife, Sybil Cutting, to create a decorative theme for the Chinese Library, named for the hand-printed silk Chinese wallpaper that decorated the room. These are Pinsent's drawings; he observed that his clients were on edge that he would not finish the work. But he did, and the library was soon completed.

Geoffrey Scott in the Boboli gardens behind the Palazzo Pitti, c. 1923, perhaps taken by Vita Sackville-West. (Courtesy of Sir Nigel Nicolson)

gardens at Sissinghurst Castle, Kent. It brought an end to his marriage to Sybil, and with it his life in Italy, and brought him to emotional as well as financial ruin. Scott wrote to Vita that he regretted having to leave Villa Medici, which, he said, had been his only home. "I'm selling everything I've got. I've nowhere to put anything if I had it." Scott requested that she be discreet about his situation and what he had become: "You can set no limits to the suffering caused to others when you smash up a life as you have mine."

•

In the decade following World War I, Pinsent's architectural vocabulary matured into a lexicon of simplified shapes enhanced by a careful development of space and form, which took its meaning from what Scott wrote about in *The Architecture of Humanism* with its notions of space and form taking precedence over historicism and decoration. Even so, he continued to have trouble resurrecting his practice. Once again Mary Berenson stepped in, hoping to send him off in a profitable direction.

In 1922 she proposed Pinsent for the position of technical adviser to the governor of Jerusalem. In a somewhat tongue-in-cheek letter to Mary thanking her for her help, Pinsent wrote that although the job sounded interesting, involving an element of building restoration, he doubted his competence to tackle such highly skilled technical enterprises as overseeing tile manufacturing, although he thought he could learn the subject, just as he had learned the fundamentals of radiology for his war work. Apart from the restoration work, there were yet other attractions to the job, and Pinsent's observations reveal what had always motivated him: "But what attracts me more than anything, is, as you rightly divine, the adventure, the breaking out into a new world and the step in a direction I have longed to go for years, namely East. And possibly a job of this sort, properly carried out, would when it came to an end, lead to others of a similar kind which might take one further East still. But this is dreaming!" "Anyhow," he added, "even if the job didn't lead to anything, I shouldn't be in anymore [sic] of a cul-de-sac than I am now, so nothing would be lost."

Part of his reluctance might have been due to the fact that his career at last seemed to be picking up. The war had interrupted his work for Strong at Villa Le Balze, and now he set about completing the library interior and decoration for the baroque stairs. According to Pinsent's index of clients, between 1921 and 1928 he executed eight major formal gardens, seven new buildings, thirty-six alterations and additions, six libraries, and two fresco projects, and made proposals for four schemes that were not carried out. His client base was not only expanding but included a number of influential people. For Sir George Sitwell he designed a library for the Sitwells' Italian castle, Montegufoni, near the town of Montagnana in Chianti. According to the late John Brandon Jones, an English architect who as a student met Pinsent in Florence, Pinsent marveled at Sitwell's requiring such an elaborate library when all he had on his shelves were paperback mysteries and crime novels. In 1926 the Italian sculptor Antonio Maraini commissioned Pinsent to carry out the conversion of a late eighteenth-century *contadino* (farmhouse) into a spacious modern villa, named Torre di Sopra (see chapter 5).

In 1929 Pinsent was consulted about creating a seaside villa, Gli Scafari, for Iris Origo's mother, Sybil Cutting Lubbock, as she now was, having married her third husband, the essayist and literary critic Percy Lubbock. (For more on Gli Scafari, see chapter 5.) Sybil, who had been in poor health for decades, found in Lubbock a caregiver—when he felt strong enough, Lubbock having his own health scares. They would remain together for nearly twenty years, until Sybil's death in 1937. Lubbock was an insular person, not given to extravagant displays of emotion of any kind, and consequently had few friends. Pinsent was one of them, and he joined the couple as they scouted for a building site. They traveled as far as the French Riviera (but Lubbock feared the region might be rife with epidemics, including dengue fever). Ultimately they settled on a parcel of land at Lerici, just south of La Spezia on the Maremma coastline. Today the fashionable resort Forti dei Marmi makes it a favorite destination of Florentine society.

•

The year 1929 also brought the death of Geoffrey Scott. Still struggling emotionally and financially, in the years after his divorce Scott slowly managed to piece together a life in London, undertaking some minor literary commissions. Other than two editions of *The Architecture of Humanism*, his only published works were a book of poems titled *A Box of Paints* (1923) and a biography of the eighteenth-century writer Madame de Charrière, *A Portrait of Zélide* (1925); a planned second volume of *The Architecture of Humanism* was never realized. His stepdaughter, Iris Origo, recalled seeing a "piece of writing paper on Scott's desk, with the words, 'A History of Taste, Volume 1, Chapter 1. It is very difficult . . . ,' inscribed neatly across the top. He never wrote any more on the subject."

In 1927, however, after active lobbying by his supporters, Scott was hired by the American collector Ralph Heywood Isham to organize and edit the private papers of James Boswell, a massive collection which Isham had, with great difficulty, acquired from Boswell's great-great-grandson. A lavish multivolume edition of the papers, to be edited by Scott and designed by the noted typographer Bruce Rogers, was announced, and Scott, who despised Americans, traveled reluctantly to New York to begin work. He was also planning to write a major biography of Boswell, and he signed a contract for this with an American firm before returning to England for several weeks in the early summer of 1929.

On August 4, 1929, after recovering from a bad case of influenza contracted while in England, Scott returned to New York

Pinsent and Scott sailed to the United States in August 1929. A month later Scott was dead and Pinsent returned to England with his ashes.

accompanied by Pinsent, whose support of his former colleague had never wavered. The two old friends cut dashing figures on the transatlantic steamer, and though they could not know it, both were at the pinnacles of their careers. Just a few weeks later Scott fell ill again with pneumonia, and on September 14 he died at the Rockefeller Institute in New York City. Pinsent was with him to the end. He helped to arrange the funeral and cremation and returned to England with Scott's ashes.

•

Pinsent was made a Fellow of the Royal Institute of British Architects in 1933. Two years later he began Villa Sparta for Queen Helen of Romania, and in 1937 he was presented with a certificate attesting to his great skill and talent as an architect, signed and presented by all the Florentine craftsmen with whom he had worked over the years. In 1938 he designed a large formal garden for Marwell Park in England, near Bournemouth. In that year too he was presented with the Order of George I, King of the Hellenes, for work carried out to royal commissions (including a racetrack and pavilion) in Athens, Tatoi, and

Certificate presented to Pinsent by the Florentine craftsmen with whom he had worked.

Piraeus. His client record shows that much of the work undertaken during the interwar years was for "decorations" such as stucco work, murals, fireplace surrounds, garden designs and hardscaping, libraries (but not on the scale of I Tatti), and additions to existing villas. New buildings were, for the most part, executed for the Origos and Lubbocks, as work for these old friends and clients of long standing was an ongoing commitment. So, though at first glance Pinsent appears to have been fully employed, the jobs were getting smaller and the client list was not expanding. Plans were presented for several large villa and garden projects, but not undertaken.

Pinsent's career was once again cut short when he left Italy shortly before the outbreak of World War II. Leaving his apartment on via delle Terme must have been gut-wrenching; his photograph album for this period has six pages devoted to his rooms there, and he documented every corner as well as the view from his window up and down the street, so that in later years he could return once again to what had been his life for thirty years. It is clear that he would have been content to die there, too, but he was compelled to leave, remarking to his family that he and the Fascists were not compatible; according to his half-brother Basil, Pinsent was not willing to cooperate with the Fascist scheme to register architects as engineers, even though he took great pride in being called *ingeniere*. But there may have been a more fundamental dissatisfaction at work; writing to Mary Berenson, he expressed his ennui as well as his ambivalence toward the new order: "What I have offered is not congenial to the time, and what the times want is not congenial to me. Or perhaps it is all just simple laziness."

Pinsent returned to England and spent the war years there, staying first with relatives from his father's side of the family in Devon, and going to Wales with his brother's ex-wife, Kitty. News from his old friends was scarce, though Iris Origo was able to remain in touch. He declined the occasional invitation to design, writing to Berenson, "But I couldn't somehow get back to building those castles in the air. All the same the feeling of wanting to get back to the old scenes and occupations is

Before Pinsent left Florence in March 1937, he carefully recorded every room and view of his apartment, the "beloved via della Terme" that had been his home for nearly three decades. These are among the twenty-nine images he carefully pasted into his photo album for that period. Top: The views up and down the street and the entrance to the dwelling; note the polyhedron finial on the baluster. Middle: The views of his office reveal models of his projects on the shelves framing the window, while views of his studio, bottom, reveal an orderly and precise environment.

On his return to England Pinsent lodged with his ex-sister-in-law, Kitty, and their friendship turned into what both hoped would be a loving companionship. But it was a lot to expect of a longtime bachelor to make room in his life for an intelligent, strong-willed woman and her two daughters, Chloe and Jane. Born Katherine Kentisbeare, the daughter of Sir George Heynes Radford and Lady Radford, Kitty Pinsent died suddenly on March, 24, 1949. Pinsent annotated the page in his album that records her death with the comment, "The best laid plans."

Pinsent, pictured in June 1940, on the porch of Lower Grange, a half-timbered farmhouse in Shillingford, for which he oversaw the renovation and modernization from 1936 to 1940 below, left, the building before, and right, after Pinsent's work was completed.

Iris sent Pinsent this photo of herself with her infant daughter, Benedetta, taken in June 1941, one year after Italy had declared war on France and England.

growing, though goodness knows if it would even be possible or would even pan out as I picture it if it were tried. Maybe this is no more than a refuge for one's thought . . . A nomad yurt and no possessions than a few pots and pans, and a partner, some-times seems the ideal."

After the Allied invasion of Italy on September 3, 1943, Pinsent was recalled to active service and went back to Florence as an officer in the Monuments, Fine Arts, and Archive Commission. It was a poignant return, as he was overseeing the preservation work on the fabric of historic Florentine villas, churches, and bridges, including salvage and mine clearance around the Ponte Vecchio. He was also involved in similar work in Milan, Bologna, and several other Italian cities, helping with recovery of displaced works of art. He was later mentioned in dispatches for having made a "substantial and profound contribution" to the preservation of Italy's artistic heritage, and a letter from an American senior officer attached to the commission added fulsome praise: "You brought to the solution of our joint problems a knowledge of Italy, and of architecture, that was as valuable as

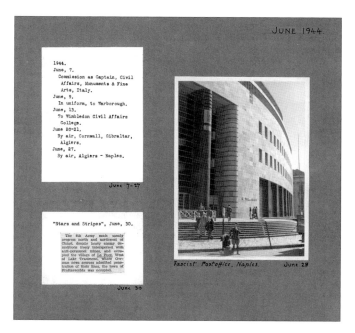

On this page, dated June 1944, Pinsent recorded his commission as a captain and his deployment into the Monuments, Fine Arts, and Archive Commission, the arrival of the 8th Army at La Foce, and the Milan post office, an example of the Fascist architecture he so despised.

Pinsent with his colleagues from the MFAA.

it was unique. To it you added a comprehension of the human spirit and of your fellow men that was to all of us not only a joy but indeed a source of very real inspiration. You have done as much good to the hearts and minds of your colleagues as you have to the bruised artistic patrimony of Italy—and that, I may add, is great."

Pinsent recorded the destruction in Florence, captioning the photograph above, left, "Bombed out houses on the south side of the Arno, above Ponte Vecchio, including what was Edmund and Mary's." Pinsent snapped the shutter for the photograph at left just as one of the historic towers was turned to rubble. Above, right, the remains of the Ponte Santa Trinità, one of the main bridges across the Arno, following Allied shelling. For the restoration, the story goes that local youths dove into the Arno to locate the statues that had graced the piers.

Inspecting Botticelli's *Primavera,* which along with other paintings from the Uffizi had been stored for safekeeping in the basement of Montegufoni, George Sitwell's villa outside Florence.

Pinsent in uniform during World War II.

MAY 1951.

Assisi. (at S. Lorenzo about Molly Berkeley's garage). May 1-5.

S.Rufino, Assisi, from bedroom window. May 2.

S.Lorenzo. New chapel complete (but for cross). May 2. assisi.

Following the war, there were opportunities to renovate damaged buildings and to repurpose some, as Pinsent did, with faint enthusiasm, for his old friend Molly Berkeley, turning a disused chapel, San Lorenzo at Assisi, into an artist's studio, shown here in 1951.

Bomb damage at Villa Le Balze, photographed by Pinsent in October 1944.

FOUR

The Last Five Seconds Before Midnight

Released from his Allied Commission duties on September 20, 1945, Pinsent stayed on in Italy for some time before returning to England in mid-1946. After a brief billet at an Oxfordshire farm, he went to Exeter in Devon, where he shared a house with his former sister-in-law, Kitty, their friendship having matured into an intimate partnership. But the arrangement with Kitty was strained, and he had no permanent home of his own, no career to which he could return, and few resources. Again, a few commissions were offered but declined. One exception was a request from an old friend, Molly Berkeley, who asked him help with the conversion of a former convent into a studio and to design a private chapel there, as she had recently converted to Catholicism. Pinsent wrote to Berenson about it: "I feel no inclination to dive into that sort of work again. The flash of conviction has gone, and in these days there is something quite unreal about turning churches into studios for female amateur painters." Worse, he was utterly dismayed by the destruction of the beauty that he had known so intimately and had in some instances helped to preserve or create. Writing to Berenson in the spring of 1946, Pinsent confessed, "It is nice to think of the international procession that flows through I Tatti to see you. It sounds very vital, compared to the vacuum that I am going through just now . . . I haven't found an occupation yet, though I need one . . . Organised public work is not in line—it makes me dry up, and for the moment the spring inside is unwound and is not pressing outwards towards anything definite. But as you say, one must let things by in times like these." And in the same letter he observed, with a note of despair, the continuing destruction, all in the name of progress:

> Town planning is the local excitement at the moment. In some cities here we are doing what we chaffed the Italians for doing, at Rimini for instance. On the strength of partial destruction grandiose plans are being made to rationalise the whole town—implying more demolition. It is all dreadfully thought out . . . and the basis is traffic, bypasses and arterial roads. I imagine the rock they will founder on will be the acquisition and demolition of standing houses or works, at a time when space of any kind, with a roof on it, is being cried out for on all sides.

One year later the situation had not improved, and Pinsent was growing ever more depressed by contemporary architectural "solutions," writing: "We are doomed for the rest of our generation to live with boxhouses and pre-fabs within sight everywhere, so I am not surprised that the picturesqueness of many Italian villages is doomed. It doesn't seem possible with the modern building methods that have to be used for economic reasons to devise anything that looks decent."

•

Geoffrey Scott's *The Architecture of Humanism: A Study in the History of Taste* is still in print today, valued for its presentation of architecture as a set of aesthetic responses expressed in terms that relate directly to the human experience. This was the "humanist" ideal, which shaped Italian architecture and garden design during the Renaissance and Baroque periods. The most significant and revolutionary aspect of Scott's theory is found in the chapter "Humanist Values," where he establishes space, mass, and line as the most important values in the interpretation of architecture, imparting reason and logic to building. Scott believed that we can most easily experience and understand architecture in terms of our movement through space, our experience of resistance and substance in mass, and our following of a linear gesture or simply the path of a line. In that way, he wrote, "we transcribe architecture into terms of ourselves." Scott also believed that the Baroque style was the one best suited to garden design because it balanced the romantic or picturesque effects established by a dramatic use of light and shade to attract and surprise, with the sense of permanence and solidity fostered by the underlying orderliness of the humanist's architectural use of space, mass, and line.

Evaluating Pinsent's early work at I Tatti and Le Balze by Scott's criteria, one can match the theory of one man to the practice of the other. At Villa Le Balze in particular, Pinsent demonstrated that he understood the dramatic deployment of mass (the villa positioned at the midpoint of the layout), line (the parallel axes that offer two very different experiences of the site), light and shade (the juxtaposed open and enclosed areas of garden and view), as they flow within architectural space. These are the essential elements that Scott recognized as being the key value of the art, the one from which our pleasure in architecture is derived, and which "the architect models in space as a sculptor in clay. He designs his space as a work of art; that is, he attempts through its means to excite a certain mood in those who enter it." Although it is unlikely that Scott had any substantial impact on the development of Pinsent's architectural language, it is quite likely that the two men exchanged ideas and respected each other's opinions. In dedicating the book to Pinsent, Scott may also have been acknowledging the value of his association with a professional architect through whom he came to understand the practice as well as the theory of architecture.

The Architecture of Humanism had huge appeal to a generation that found the cool rationale of the classical orders more attractive than the fervid emotional responses to architectural forms espoused by Ruskin. Scott's debunking of Ruskinian thought as the "four fallacies" was influential, and among the converted was the English art historian and critic Sir Kenneth Clark. In *The*

Gothic Revival (1928) he followed Scott's line in assessing Ruskin. (Twenty-two years later, in the second edition, Clark wrote, "Scott's powers of lucid exposition had blinded me to the fundamental unreality of his position.")

•

Pinsent's disdain for the direction of postwar modernism was rooted in his training as an Arts and Crafts architect, where materials and forms were handled with a respect sometimes bordering on reverence, and where the simplicity and appropriateness of a design to its site and use were the paramount consideration in the architect's approach. In the postwar period there was no time for such deliberation; the mechanization of building dictated the aesthetic. A successful modern building by Pinsent's criteria was one that was perfect in all its details, and few modernist buildings lived up to those high standards.

Yet despite his waning interest in architecture, a flicker of his creative urge remained, and Pinsent found various ways to satisfy it, describing to Berenson his latest hobbies:

> The slackness—war aftermath—seems at last to be passing off, and a desire to create something is returning. I have marked time all last year with a hobby making a relief map . . . the attempt to write was a washout. Pictures, preferably solid, are my medium, not words, so I am embarking on a series of model stage scenes, not for the stage, but fantasies depicted and set up in the model stage scene method. This combines invention, painting, and building but without the responsibility; and if unsuccessful can be immediately destroyed unlike bricks and mortar which stand and reproach you (nine time out of ten) for the rest of your life.

These artfully constructed scenes recall Pinsent's way of presenting architectural proposals as three-dimensional models fashioned from plasticine clay—a direct expression of his concern with space and mass. The English architect John Brandon

Jones described seeing one of these models in Pinsent's studio at via della Terme:

> I was very interested in the way he designed to a considerable extent by making plasticine models [probably these didn't survive] because you just squeezed them up to do the next model . . . But he had a couple of "sites" on hand when we went up to his office, and he had been working on them. There was not a lot of detail; they weren't like these silly models people make now, where instead of appreciating the building you wonder how on earth the model-maker made the railings so small . . . These were just chunky blocks carved with a penknife or plasterer's trowel, showing the villa, terraces, gardens, . . . about as big as a large drawing board.

In the late summer of 1948, Pinsent went on a month-long tour in Switzerland with Kitty—the seemingly on-again-off-again nature of their relationship had been a strain for both, yet Pinsent seemed willing to make an effort for it succeed, and this trip may have been an attempt to mend fences. The trip, he wrote to Berenson in October, "roused an interest in geology and some of our excursions were to this end. I got hold of an elementary book on the geology of Switzerland, and have been filling my spare time in translating it from German to English." Architecture remained on his mind, and in a flurry of optimism he sent for the rules of an international competition for a new palace at Addis Ababa for the emperor of Ethiopia: "a really 'unlikely' thing, just up my street." But the scheme turned out to be too enormous to undertake single-handed and get done in time, so "regretfully, I let it go . . . ten or fifteen years ago I would have plunged in recklessly."

Pinsent traveled to Scotland and stayed in a grand baronial building designed by William Wallace, the architect to whom, as he explained to Berenson, "my father articled me at the beginning of my career before I had ever even heard of you and when Italy was still a mythical country across the mountains." He confessed, "It was slightly nightmarish to be confronted with such a solid and forbidding ghost! It made me realize what an enormous part chance plays in determining the direction of one's life."

After Kitty's sudden death in early 1949, which caused Pinsent to reveal his regret at not being able to make a success of their relationship, he moved to Bournemouth, to the house he had built for Jane Houghton. Mary Houghton had died in February 1942, and Edmund was living alone in his late sister's house on St. Anthony's Road. Just as he had found it "nightmarish" to be staying in a baronial hall with the ghost of his early master, so Pinsent thought it a cruel irony to be living in the first house he had ever designed.

Throughout these years, Pinsent kept up a steady correspondence with Berenson and returned annually to visit him and Iris Origo. The wave of postwar modernization taking place in the ancient cities of Italy under the guise of restoration and conservation was of great concern to both Pinsent and Berenson, who addressed himself to the problem in an unpublished essay titled "How to Rebuild Florence." His solution was to call upon the archetypal memory—the "spontaneous evocation" held by people all over the world, of the birthplace of the Renaissance—and thereby avoid the transformation of Florence into something aesthetically and spiritually devalued, whether by wholesale demolition of historic areas or by cultivating areas of destruction as romantic, picturesque ruins. In Berenson's estimation, as the world had once looked to Florence as a cultural avatar, so it would look again, and whatever scheme Florence pursued for the rehabilitation of its ancient fabric, so the civilized world would follow:

> Florence has a responsibility to the rest of Italy, and perhaps to the European world in every part of the globe owing to an indisputable fact in art history . . . that wherever European influence goes it takes not only to all the Americas, but to India and China, to Japan, an architecture that no matter how developed and transformed by movement and latent requirements, an architecture and urban landscape that were worked out by Florentines and their pupils from elsewhere, in the fifteenth and sixteenth

centuries. In no other art has Florence influenced the world so much, not even in painting or in sculpture.

Pinsent's unease with the new order was no doubt compounded by the fact that, having spent his entire professional career and most of his maturity in Italy, on returning to England he felt an alien in his own country. His annual trips to Florence were, as he explained to Berenson, in effect a personal pilgrimage; I Tatti and La Foce he recognized as being "the scenes of my most poignant experiences."

Pinsent's dissatisfaction with modernism—and disdain for its practitioners—and his postwar ennui disconnected him from architecture. The art historian John Fleming recalled that Pinsent "had really enjoyed being an architect and he enjoyed architecture; it was a toy and he loved to play with it." After the war, however, he was "out of step with everybody else—and the modern movement. Like the popular English architect Edwin Lutyens, Pinsent worked entirely in his own way; he had a small practice for very rich clients, and after the war these clients were fewer.

Among these few clients was Contessa Flavia della Gherardesca, for whom, in 1948, he designed a *tempietto*, or memorial chapel, set in a forest clearing near Bolgheri in Livorno. A long dressed-stone path leads to the circular, domed structure, which is elevated on a stone-built platform. In a clearing behind the chapel, two unadorned slabs indicate the Gheradesca graves; this area is bordered by stone curbing and there are two simple seats for resting places. Pines and cypresses, gorse, and shrubby herbs embrace the site. The location is slightly elevated, enough to enable a glimpse of the distant sea from the platform. It is an appealing rendition of a classical temple set in a sylvan glade, with all the grace and dignity such a monument demands. On its completion Pinsent wrote to Berenson, "The *tempietto* at Bolgheri looked harsh and new, but I felt the proportions and details were all right and that it would acquire dignity with time." This remark recalls the statement made by C. E. Mallows some fifty years earlier, with regard to landscape gardens: "Time so often obliterates the mistakes of men."

Three years later, Pinsent designed one of his final garden-memorials. At Skipwith Hall in Yorkshire, he planned a shelter garden as a memorial for a grandson of Irene Forbes Adams (née Lawley) who had died in a drowning accident. It is a somber little brick enclosure, and not one of his most inspired efforts, but then Pinsent's ill health was taking a severe toll on his energy,

Contemporary views of the Gheradesca *tempietto*. (Ethne Clarke)

Flavia della Gherardesca's memorial tempietto to Gogo going up at Bolgheri. Sept. 15, 1948. (Photos sent by Flavia)

FEB. 1949.

Flavia della Gherardesca's memorial tempietto to Gogo, at Bolgheri, complete but for cross.

1 Feb. 1949. (Photos sent by Nina)

Two pages from Pinsent's album illustrate the construction of the Gheradesca *tempietto*. Wooden scaffolding, logs used to roll the lintel into position, and in the background the pair of white oxen used to haul the building materials to the site. Although the memorial is now surrounded by a thicket of trees and shrubs, it originally had an imposing position in the countryside.

and it added to his general disaffection with architecture, garden design—and life in England.

In 1950 he designed the library extension for the Fototeca at I Tatti. Luisa Vertova Nicolson, who was then the librarian, recalls coming upon Pinsent in the library and asking if he needed assistance; Pinsent quietly explained that he was simply trying to establish if the space "worked," something that could be done only when it was being used for the purpose for which it was designed—in other words, that a room did not exist except for the people within it.

Edmund Houghton died on September 6, 1953, and the next day Pinsent wrote to Berenson, "He was the first person, after a stuffy and strict home-upbringing, to open windows onto new horizons for me, and to show that there were more ways than one of living a reasonable life." To his half-brother Basil he later remarked, "I went to Italy with the Houghtons for six weeks for holiday and I ended up staying 30 years."

Not long after Houghton's death Pinsent moved to Hilterfingen Thunersee, Switzerland, where he lodged with the family of Elisabeth (Bethly) Laderach, former nanny to Kitty Pinsent's children, Chloe and Jane. There had been some discussion that he might live in Sheffield with Chloe and her husband, Ian Morton,

Pinsent photographed I Tatti in April 1951, when the garden was forty-two years old.

and their young family, but the circumstances of that arrangement were unsatisfactory for a fastidious elderly man, distracted by the urban decay of postwar Britain. Besides, while living on the farm in Warborough, Oxfordshire, after leaving the service, he discovered that he had enjoyed the simple life of farm families; it had been an especially comfortable and happy time for him and he decided to recapture it.

In the mid-1950s Pinsent made a trip to the United States with his niece Jane. They drove across the country from New York to Santa Barbara, where Pinsent stayed with two of Berenson's sisters for a few weeks before returning to England. Jane recalls that Pinsent enjoyed stopping at roadside diners, not for the food but because of the colloquial banter between the wait staff, cooks, and customers. He had always had an appreciation of local dialects and prided himself on his ability to speak with craftsmen and laborers in the vernacular. Of all the experiences on the journey, Pinsent was most interested in the variety of the geological formations he observed while crossing the country. Throughout his creative life Pinsent had been absorbed by the relationship of the built and natural landscape, and had translated his observations into the plan and construction of his buildings and gardens. "I cannot find anyone to tell me—without calling in Einsteinian mathematics—why one crystal chooses to grow in hairs as thin as ours, while another grows in blocks or thick slabs," he wrote to Berenson in 1953. "Not knowing, and therefore trying to find out is the great thing, and there seems to be as endless and proportionally fascinating supply of things not known in this subject."

So it seems that in his final project, the construction of a collection of ninety-nine models illustrating the elements of crystallography, Pinsent was carrying on a search for the underlying geometric order of the world. He had suffered a series of mild strokes and developed a tremor in his right arm. To enable him to complete the models, he devised a brace to steady his hand and tools to aid his grip. He maintained his agile and inquiring mind to the end, observing to his niece Chloe that living a simple life with Laderach's family in Hilterfingen had brought him much contentment, and that he had enjoyed watching the village grow

Los Angeles station, Calif. Stainless steel railroad carriages. June 23.

Grand Canyon, Ariz. Looking across from near El Tovar hotel. Thick haze. June 24.

Grand Canyon. Looking down valley from near El Tovar hotel. June 24

Grand Canyon. Looking up valley from near El Tovar hotel. June 24

Snapshots from the motor trip across the United States Pinsent made with his niece Jane. He recorded landscape (top, the Grand Canyon), geological formations, vernacular buildings, suburban housing, a gang of cowboys on a cattle drive in Montana, and, above, Senda Berenson, Bernard's sister, and her friend outside their California bungalow.

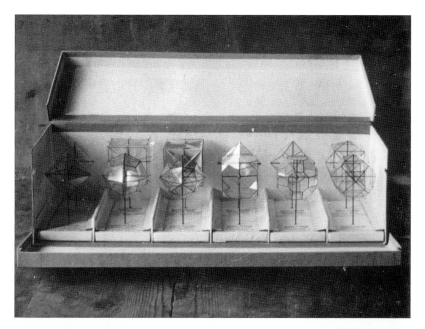

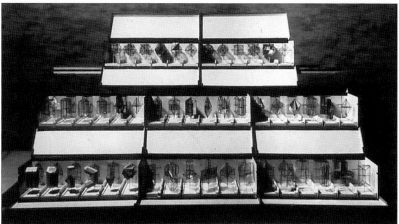

Crystal models crafted by Pinsent

and the seasons change in the Swiss mountains where he had spent time as a young man. As Jane recalls, her uncle was quite dismissive of his work, claiming that it was, in the great scheme of things, unimportant. In 1956, after reading Berenson's memoir, *Sketch for a Self-Portrait,* Pinsent wrote to him of his own life, now being led in rural obscurity: "My life is not all calm and content-ment. I have my little dilemmas too! A little goblin sometimes whispers to me that vanity may be an ingredient; not being able to impress the world with my greatness, I retire to a place where there is no world to impress."

Until Berenson's death on October 6, 1959, he and Pinsent were regular correspondents, exchanging not only news of their

Living in quiet retirement in Switzerland, Pinsent savored the calm order of his life. He enjoyed watching the neighbor's children play, taking coffee on the terrace of the town's main hotel (where he surprised a team of Italian roadmenders by speaking to them in fluent, idiomatic Italian), and attending the annual "Tracht" or folk festival, where he posed for a souvenir photo with a "bear."

Pinsent as a young man, perched on a cross in the Alps during a rest stop on one of his youthful hiking trips through Switzerland.

daily lives and changing interests, but also meditations on their mortality: "I don't see why the prospect of extinction should be impossible for you to enjoy," Pinsent wrote to Berenson in 1954. "My own belief is that there will be no 'I' then, so am inclined to make the most of the possibilities now, while there is one"—which he did by nurturing his innate sense of curiosity about the natural world and the man's need to credit his existence to some greater external being. Pinsent ended this particularly philosophical letter by marveling at what he referred to as the "time-band theory" of the creation of earth, with man's evolution "being the last five seconds before midnight."

Pinsent's last five seconds came on Thursday, December 5, 1963, and he was buried in the churchyard at Hilterfingen.

View of Florence from Villa Gamberaia. Of all the villas dotting the hillsides around the city, none was more admired and emulated than the Villa Gamberaia. One of the key tenets of Renaissance design was formulated by Gianbattista Alberti, who in his writings on architecture advised that a hillside position, which gave exposure to healthful breezes and provided a view of the city, was the ideal setting for a humanist villa and garden. (Ethne Clarke)

FIVE

A Sense of
the Informing Spirit

Cecil Pinsent's beginnings as an architect coincided with a country-house building boom, as the nouveaux riches of the Industrial Age commissioned lavish houses and landscaped parks and gardens, traditionally the emblem of hereditary wealth, as highly visible symbols of their new economic (if not social) status. Similarly, the newly wealthy pursued old-money traditions in the style of their buildings, and late seventeenth- and eighteenth-century classicism became the preferred stylistic idiom, although expressed in many ways, such as the Italianate manner, with its deference to classical orders, and the more decorative, French-influenced Beaux-Arts style. There were, however, clients willing to finance the construction of picturesque Arts and Crafts manor houses, such as those being built in the Cotswolds by the Barnsley brothers and in Surrey by Edwin Lutyens (who later abandoned the rural-vernacular manor house in favor of a more classically styled building when it became evident that such a style was more attractive to prospective clients).

Along with the dominance of classical orders in architecture came the revival of the formal, geometrically ordered garden, whose seventeenth-century forms were made familiar through the popularizing work of Blomfield's *The Formal Garden in England* (1892) and Sedding's *Garden-craft Old and New* (1891). Each author maintained that only an architect was equipped to design a garden, for, as Pinsent's employer C. E. Mallows believed, the garden was by its nature an extension of the house; it was in essence an architectural space in which hedges formed the walls, the sky defined the ceiling, and manicured lawns established the floor. Clipped topiary in geometric forms and lavish flower borders provided the furnishings. Blomfield's and Sedding's books were among the first post-eighteenth-century works to examine the lost formal gardens of England, and to assert that the origins of the style could be found in the Renaissance gardens of Italy.

As the "Battle of the Styles" worked itself out, it came to be seen that less formal plantings characteristic of the so-called wild garden had a role to play in the classically designed garden, and working from this premise Gertrude Jekyll, collaborating with Edwin Lutyens, completed some of the most memorable house and landscape combinations, setting out the formal plan/informal planting formula that became the hallmark of twentieth-century English garden design. As the landscape historian David Ottewill writes, "One of [Jekyll and Lutyens's] earliest masterpieces, Deanery Garden, Berkshire (1899), was laid out within an existing

An engraving by Giuseppe Zocchi (fl. 1744) of the Villa Gamberaia, part of a series of *vedute,* or views, of all the notable Florentine villas, commissioned by his patron the Marchese Gerini.

walled garden where the axes of the house are projected outwards to form routes and vistas, thus making the house appear larger than it is, as at Villa Gamberaia." Ottewill goes on to liken the formal plan of this garden, with its quasi-Tudor style, to that of Tirley Garth, by C. E. Mallows, Pinsent's one-time master.

It was to Pinsent's advantage that in working, however briefly, with Mallows, he had been exposed to the principles of formal garden design and the idea of the Italian Renaissance garden as the template for perfection in landscape. He was, therefore, ideally placed to satisfy the architectural and landscape needs of the Anglo-American émigrés to Florence, whose goal, as the Italian garden historian Vincenzo Cazzato describes it, was to rediscover, if possible, the original form of an old garden and then restore it (a goal seldom achieved), or to implement, in either restoration or new construction, the proper elements of plan and ornament for a garden *all'italiana*. This revivalist approach, while seductive, was, as Cazzato points out, rarely authentic.

In Pinsent's hands, however, the historic language of the style was subtly expressed; in all his garden plans, box and cypress hedges lack the overbearing dimensions of their Victorian English counterparts, and they are instead used to delicately frame views or repeat the historic models (in the case of garden renovation). Beds are kept simple, often filled with turf studded over with wild meadow flowers, violets and daisies and the like, as though the ground were the model for an early Renaissance painting. Container-grown citrus, roses, and other flowering shrubs accent walkways and transition points in the plan. Thus, in his command of a historic style of landscape design, expressed through his own peculiar architectural syntax, he developed a style that can be recognized, "in its own right, rather than as mere eclecticism." In this respect, Pinsent seems to have absorbed the advice of Edith Wharton, whose view was that while the form of Italian gardens was praiseworthy, it was their spirit that should be followed rather than the letter of their plan and ornament. Sir George Sitwell, too, in the preface to his *On the Making of Gardens* (1909), which was aimed at shifting the direction of garden design toward the formal style, wrote, "If the world is to make great gardens again,

The water parterre at Villa Gamberaia was created in the early twentieth century on the site of the old parterre garden, which, when Edith Wharton saw it in 1903 while researching her book *Italian Villas and Their Gardens,* was still a vegetable garden tended by the farmers who had been squatting in the old villa. The water garden was installed by Princess Ghyka, who owned the villa in early 1900s, after Wharton's visit. This view dates from the 1930s.

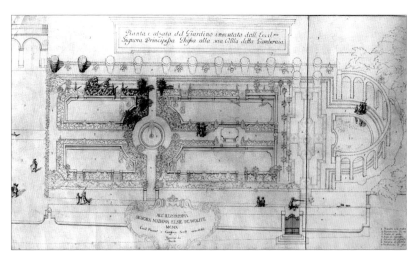

Pinsent's drawing for the water parterre, dated 1910, is inscribed to the American interior designer Elsie de Wolfe (Lady Mendl) and labeled as being "after Zocchi"; Princess Ghyka was de Wolfe's patron. As Pinsent did not include any work at Villa Gamberaia in his list of clients, it is unlikely that he had any part in the design of the garden feature.

The Villa Gamberaia today. (Ethne Clarke)

we must both discover and apply in the changed circumstances of modern life the principles which guided the garden-makers of the Renaissance, and must be ready to learn all that science can teach us concerning the laws of artistic presentment."

Pinsent himself seems never to have written anything for publication about the practice of architecture or his approach or aesthetic, but he did write about the theory and practice of garden design for *Il giardino fiorito*, a magazine started by Iris Origo while she and Pinsent were working on the gardens at La Foce, with the aim of raising an awareness of the art and practice of garden-making and horticulture among the Italian community. It was an attractive publication, with solid articles on plants and notable gardens, and in 1931 Pinsent contributed "Giardini moderni all'italiana" (Modern Gardens in the Italian Style). The article reveals several aspects of his mature approach to architecture and landscape: that he was well aware of honoring historical context without falling victim to historicism, that he well understood and was able to translate the traditions of Renaissance garden planning into a contemporary style to suit the needs of his clients, and that he had working knowledge of the trees, shrubs, and flowers best suited to cultivation in "modern" Italian gardens. "The modern stylized garden," he wrote, "should have order and dignity in the area nearest to the house, so that the view from the window provides a calm and restful experience." But he advised that the more "frivolous" parts of the garden scheme were best kept at some distance from the house to heighten the pleasure of their discovery, while "more practical, less stylized elements" were to be relegated to the edge of the garden. All of this is in keeping with Gertrude Jekyll's and C. E. Mallows's recommendations for good garden design and planning. (For further excerpts from "Giardini moderni all'italiana," see Appendix B.)

•

My discussion of Pinsent's work focuses on four of his earliest projects, as these are the ones that established his credentials: his first commission at St. Anthony's Road, Bournemouth, for Jane Houghton, a straightforward Arts and Crafts dwelling with Italianate overtones, undertaken just as he was relocating to Italy in 1907; the Villa I Tatti, for the Berensons, upon which Pinsent's architectural career in Tuscany was built; the Villa Le Balze, for Charles Augustus Strong, an example of Pinsent's early mastery of site and vernacular; and La Foce, for Iris and Antonio Origo, which demonstrates his ability to interpret the needs and desires of a client through his own fluent architectural vocabulary. A final gathering of two other representative projects from the 1920s gives an idea of the range of his talent. Pinsent considered himself an architect, but as a consequence of his training in the Arts and Crafts oeuvre, he incorporated landscape design within his self-definition. For this reason my descriptions of the gardens Pinsent created also touch on the architectural element of each with regard to its role in the overall plan.

20 St Anthony's Road, Bournemouth

In 1907, the same year that Pinsent returned to Italy to resume work on an unidentified project, a commission received on his first foray into Tuscany, he also executed a small house with formal gardens at 20 St. Anthony's Road, Bournemouth. His client was Miss Jane Houghton, Edmund Houghton's sister, who was, according to their cousin Jill Houghton, a well-educated, widely traveled spinster of independent means and mind. The St. Anthony's Road house is significant: of the few that Pinsent executed during his active career, this was the very first full-blown design-and-build architectural project that included a garden, and the first undertaken for a discerning client with whom he had, or later came to have, a lasting and in many cases devoted friendship. St. Anthony's Road featured throughout Pinsent's life: commissioned by his first love's aunt, whose brother Edmund inspired Pinsent's move to Italy, it was where he turned for refuge when his life in Italy ended, as he moved into the house with Edmund and lived there until his old friend's death. For someone like Pinsent, used to the glamorous seaside resorts of the Italian and French Mediterranean coasts, Bournemouth, with its fish-

Above and left, Miss Jane Houghton, Pinsent's first client for a design-and-build project, a small house and garden in Bournemouth, England. She was the sister of Pinsent's mentor, Edmund Houghton, and aunt to his fiancée, Alice Houghton.

and-chip stalls, bingo halls, and other pedestrian amenities, must have been less than stimulating. But when he built the house, he was about to step into a world of creative energy he had up until then only sampled. Echoes of his experiences are evident in some of the decoration at St. Anthony's, but by and large it is a solidly built little house, reserved and well-mannered like its owner, but capable of surprising twists.

The house is the smallest in a street of large Arts and Crafts houses, built on spacious plots in what is now a conservation area in Bournemouth known as "The Saints." The client list Pinsent compiled in 1955 itemizes the plan and construction of a formal garden for this property. It is sited on a corner plot and built on a north–south axis; the interior is arranged so that all the liv-

The simple lines and clean façade of Pinsent's first domestic building hint at the direction he followed for his more substantial commissions later in life. (Ethne Clarke)

ing, dining, and bedrooms are along the south-facing front, with the entrance to the sunken garden from this side, while the hall, stairs, servants' rooms, and other functional rooms are along the north. A wooden pergola over the doors from the south-facing drawing room leads into what was once the main garden, which vanished when that part of the property was sold for development in 1971. A remnant of the original main axial path ends at the new perimeter fence, and close examination of photographs taken by Edmund Houghton reveals what appear to be extensive herbaceous borders and a Chinoiserie gazebo.

The understated simplicity of the house exterior is keenly balanced by the ingenuity of the interior details that are elegant in their scale and relationship. The street façade is unadorned, its bland visage giving no hint of the lively treatment of the south-

Houghton's photograph of the interior of Jane Houghton's villa shows the Arts and Crafts detailing, with William Morris tiles around the fireplace and a few select pieces of English oak furniture.

A 1939 photograph by Cecil Pinsent shows Mary Houghton, Jane Houghton's sister-in-law, at a cottage window in Oxfordshire.

Edmund Houghton's photograph of the garden façade shows a distinct Italianate feel in the graceful curve of the loggia and its colonnade and the use of white linen drapes to provide shade.

facing aspect, which is symmetrical, with a bowed two-story gable centered above a loggia of stone Tuscan-style columns. Beneath the loggia there is a sunken garden built around a formal, stone-edged pool shaped to repeat the outward curve of the loggia. This is an enclosed, almost secret garden, designed to enhance an uninspiring site and as many sunny days as there are in this quintessential English seaside town. The structure's modesty and lack of pretension make a telling statement about Pinsent's early ability to signify a client's character through his or her dwelling, particularly when set against his first major Italian commission for the illustrious Mr. and Mrs. Bernard Berenson.

Villa I Tatti, Settignano

Not long after he returned to Florence in October 1907, Pinsent accepted the Berensons as clients, and in May 1909 he became their architect, overseeing the I Tatti renovations. It was a huge undertaking for such a comparative newcomer to the profession. The Berensons' willingness to commission someone with limited experience reflects to some degree their expatriate desire to work with an English architect, someone who spoke their language and who shared their vision. Of course, it may well have saved them money, and it certainly served Mary Berenson's specific need to find work for her protégé, Geoffrey Scott. Nevertheless, the young and relatively inexperienced Pinsent was all too often the target of the Berensons' anger.

For two years Pinsent worked at I Tatti almost exclusively, with Scott only infrequently in attendance. The main structure was in a near-desolate state and lacked every modern convenience, which at the time meant there was no plumbing worthy of the name and certainly no indoor sanitation. Olive groves and grape vines clung to the crumbling terraces. There was no trace of a garden. Pinsent's task was to transform this ill-groomed farmhouse into a gentleman's well-appointed estate that would in time reflect Bernard Berenson's growing stature as an authority on Italian Renaissance art. The villa also came to symbolize his imperious character. Looking at I Tatti today through the historical lens of Berenson's biography, the villa floats above a cascade of manicured box-edged terraces, the scene punctuated by a tasteful scattering of fountains and classical statuary; it has faint but distinct echoes of the splendor of the Villa d'Este at Tivoli outside Rome, where terraced gardens with lavish water features descend the hillside from the ducal palace sited on the crown of the hill. It is easy to imagine that Berenson might well have felt comfortable in that setting, too.

Mary Berenson's granddaughter Barbara Strachey remarks that while Pinsent had good ideas for the new library at I Tatti (and the library was at the core of the project, supporting Berenson's erudition and research), he found it difficult to control the Italian workmen. This may have been what led Pinsent to master the various craft skills, such as pebble mosaic work, needed to ornament his designs, since that was the most effective method he could find of showing the craftsmen precisely what he wanted. Apart from that, Pinsent's Arts and Crafts background allied to his active curiosity (overactive, according to his friends and family) may also have contributed to his jack-of-all-trades approach.

Pinsent liked to take a problem or technique and single-handedly tease out all he could; his thoroughness in that respect often led clients to regard him as lazy and easily distracted. They were not entirely off the mark. Mary Berenson's letters to her family catalog the disasters and successes of the transformation of I Tatti, and they also give insights into Pinsent's method of working, which at this early stage of his career revealed a hesitant approach. This gave his working methods the appearance of procrastination, as if he was putting off the execution of a project for fear of its likely failure. In 1913, Mary wrote to her family:

> He has strange periods of purposeless activity, when he will sit up all night to get a new sort of clip fastened onto his old piles of letters, or a new kind of cut in the papers that mask their photographs, or some such futility. These fits overtake him just when his clients' affairs have reached the moment psychologique when he can either finish things on time and get the details to suit them, or when by

A postcard sent by Edith Wharton to Henry James in October 1911 shows the Villa I Tatti with improvements just under way. (Courtesy of Beinecke Library, Rare Books and Manuscript Library, Yale University)

delaying he throws everything behindhand, scamps the details, rushes through the work at double pace and extra pay, gives his clients the idea of disorder and inattention, enrages and despairs them, and undoes or rather negates in their minds all the really good work he had done up to this point. This is the just the moment when his partner is or could be very valuable, for Geoffrey foresees everything that people will feel, he understands the psychological effect that will be produced. And he does not fail to tell Cecil, and sometimes it does good. But Cecil is a human eel-monkey and slips out of his grasp and chatters in a tree, so to speak.

Procrastinators will recognize that it is often only by distracting themselves with one activity that they can resolve the course of action in another—reputedly a common trait of the creative mind.

•

The Villa I Tatti is located about four miles northeast of Florence in the hillside village of Settignano; the sixteenth-century villa and its outbuildings encompass gardens and farmland of more than seventy-five acres. The villa is situated on the crest of a low hill, and the main Settignano–Florence road runs close by its front, east-facing aspect. At the west-facing side of the villa there is a *pensile* garden (a garden raised above ground level), partially enclosed by tall stuccoed walls and planted with a box-edged parterre.

Pinsent sited the main garden on the south side of the villa to descend the hillside in a series of stepped terraces, the entrance to which is framed by an arched passage he created from an old *limonaia*, which had been used to store the lemon trees, but which Pinsent repurposed as an outdoor room where Berenson could receive guests, lecture students, or just quietly sit and sip tea. From the vantage point of the *limonaia* and the balcony of a small double staircase that leads into the garden, the main axial path sweeps down the hill through the box-trimmed terraces to end at a shallow reflecting pool; looking up, a distant view of Florence and the hills beyond the city shimmers above a pedestal formed by the clipped crowns of ilex and cypress. The bright distant view is apparent only from this topmost garden level. As one walks further down the path, one is drawn into the garden, cloistered by the shadows of tall cypress and oak hedges; the Baroque drama of light and shade is immediately evident, producing a chiaroscuro effect enhanced by the monochromatic greenness of the garden where no flower color is allowed. It is an elegant exercise in garden theatre.

The east and west sides of the terrace are planted with double cypress allées, forming dark shaded tunnels where Berenson took his daily walks. The east-side allée was planted along the path of the old road, which was moved to accommodate its inclusion in the garden plan. A postcard sent by Pinsent to a friend on April 25, 1951, shows this avenue; Pinsent's message reads, "I planted this avenue of cypresses (part of a big Italian garden) in 1909." What he did not mention was that his unfamiliarity with

The *pensile* garden outside the library entrance at I Tatti sets the stage for the interior and the elegant sequencing of halls and doorways leading to the library itself. (Ethne Clarke)

Views of the terraced garden at I Tatti in 1950 (top), 2001, middle, and 2009, after the renovation of the small ilex grove at the foot of the terrace garden lowered the canopy to reveal the view and more closely respond to Pinsent's original intention to provide an evergreen frame.
(Ethne Clarke, middle and bottom)

transplanting large trees caused many of them to blow down in a strong wind. (Mary felt she and Bernard were at least partly to blame for this early fiasco, "for giving so young and inexperienced and cocksure a man such a free hand.")

Berenson had Pinsent plan the paths through the garden so that he could easily take long walks through a variety of gently transitioning landscape scenes and moods, following a choice of routes, subtly suggested not by gates or fences but by changes in style or topography. Work on the property progressed steadily, and in late 1911, with Pinsent in good graces with the Berensons, Mary was able to declare the all-important library he had designed "a dream," and the house as clean and tidy "as a jewel." The following year, however, Pinsent had fallen from grace, and Mary was bemoaning the fact that costs had spiraled out of control and blaming it all on Pinsent's inability to "run on the rails of common sense." Yet, she persisted in supporting the "Artichokes" as she called the young architects, defending them when Bernard was ready to send them both packing for having committed some new unforgivable transgression.

Pinsent, for his part, was beginning to realize that his business partner was more of a notion than a fact, and was considering how much more professional it would be for him to execute the commissions on his own, rather than spend time coddling Mary's protégé. So determined was she to keep Scott employed that she went so far as to encourage his crush on her daughter Karin, with whom, during her visit to I Tatti in April 1912, Scott had become smitten. Scott became so lovesick after she left that he was unable to work, and when Mary wrote, urging her to return to I Tatti, she observed, "Cecil works very hard, and Geoffrey practically doesn't work at all: I think it is really becoming serious as regards Cecil . . . and what would he do if Cecil suddenly turned and said, 'See here, you don't do your share and I see you won't, so we had better part.'"

Bernard Berenson's reputation was that of an arrogant and impatient man, and he often blamed Mary for I Tatti's enormous cost. The financial picture was no brighter in 1916, when Mary wrote to her sister, Alys, fretting about the renovations having

The Cypress Walk was one of Berenson's favorite areas of the garden, and one that provided Pinsent with his first experience of failed garden planting: the young trees were blown over in a storm as he had not given them adequate support. (Ethne Clarke)

A view of I Tatti, taken in 1911, showing the cypress avenue and "garden growing up," as Pinsent notes. These are the small, rather fuzzy looking trees along the right edge of photograph, not the mature cypresses framing the limonaia.

gone very much over budget. But, as Mary was always able to do, she found a way to justify the expense, saying, with what amounts to honesty and insight, "The elegance and grandeur of this house is BB's wish, though also mine (to give work to the architects)."

In the early years of his association with Pinsent, Berenson frequently criticized the young architect for his lack of common sense and ability. The art historian Sir Kenneth Clark, who was Berenson's secretary during the 1920s, later wrote that Berenson had always disliked the "imitation Baroque garden" built by "Mary Berenson under Pinsent's influence." It is true that Cecil was asked to redo the design for the clock tower (a baroque-inspired addition to the villa's main garden façade, constructed at Mary's insistence to Pinsent's design) as neither of the Berensons was satisfied. On April 11, 1927, Mary wrote to her sister Alys that Bernard, shaking his fists and fuming as he left the Library, accused Mary of "killing him by inches" and Pinsent of having done nothing he liked, and raged that he could no longer stand the life Mary "made him lead." Mary blamed her husband's black mood on the new garden walk and clock tower: "Your one idea," she quotes him as saying, "is to give that insolent unbearable Cecil something to do." Yet Berenson wrote in his memoirs, "Although I had so gifted an architect as Pinsent, who often understood my wants better than I did, it half killed me to get it into shape . . . [N]ow after many years I love it as much as one can love any object or complex of objects not human."

Villa Le Balze, Fiesole

As the main part of Pinsent's work remodeling I Tatti was nearing completion, he received his first commission to design and build a new villa and garden at a site in Fiesole. The client was Charles Augustus Strong, an American expatriate and a patron of the philosopher Georges Santayana; as Harvard students, both men had been friends with Berenson and Charles Loeser (an American art collector who also settled in Florence, for whom Pinsent had made a proposal for a loggia extension at his Tuscan villa). Strong had reputedly considered Frank Lloyd Wright as his architect, and was looking at a particular tract of land in Fiesole, but both architect and site were found to be unobtainable, and so Strong enlisted Pinsent and Scott to advise on a new location and the creation of an appropriate dwelling. Strong was a philosopher man-

Le Balze: elevation drawing by Cecil Pinsent

Le Balze: elevation photograph, c. 1957

qué, an author and scholar; he pursued a quiet, contemplative, and (following the death of his wealthy wife) seemingly monastic life. Pinsent threw himself into the work and in April 1912 presented his drawings to Strong.

The Le Balze commission was seminal to Pinsent's development as an architect, giving him his first major commission for a new structure on a difficult site. The topography of the site is challenging; the villa and garden are set on a level shelf midway down a precipitous slope with the parallel axes of the garden flowing in front of the villa and behind it. The layout of the garden is such that the distant views of the Arno valley and Florence are not fully disclosed until the furthest point of the garden is reached. The garden spaces are small individual enclosures, each with a character distinct from its neighbor, so that this contained

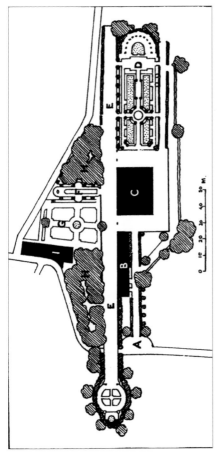

Pinsent drew this plan of the Villa Gamberaia in 1911, while he was working on the plan for Villa Le Balze, and just one year after he prepared the drawing of the water parterre for Elsie de Wolfe (see page 110). Gamberaia can't have been far from his mind while he developed the scheme for Le Balze.

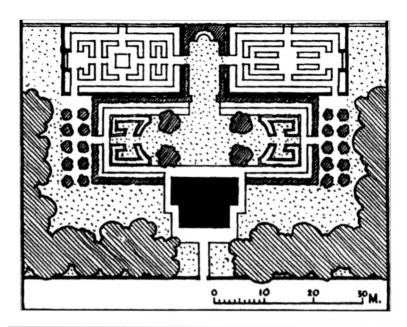

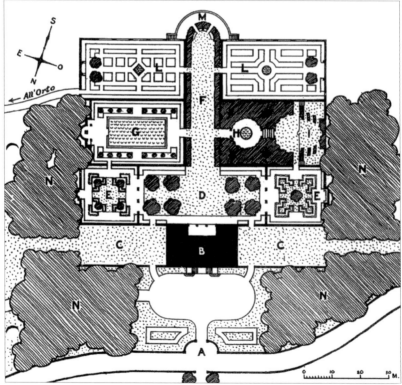

Two plans for ideal gardens prepared by Pinsent to illustrate his principles of good garden design, as set out in an article he wrote for *Il giardino fiorito*.

and controlled garden seems much more spacious and irregular than it is in reality. In its totality, and in the simplicity with which Pinsent resolved the program for a complex site, it appears that he completely assimilated the lessons learned from C. E. Mallows, who in his article "Architectural Gardening" observed, "The designers [during the Renaissance] considered the whole problem of the house design and distribution of the various parts of the ground surrounding it as one complete work, where each detail took its right place as an indispensable part of the whole."

Moreover, Le Balze is possibly the best example of Pinsent's innate ability at placing buildings within the landscape, a quality he admired in the plan and placement of the historic Villa Gamberaia, in nearby Settignano. One of the few garden drawings to survive in Pinsent's archive is the photographic print of the plan of the water parterre at Villa Gamberaia. The plan is inscribed to Elsie de Wolfe for Princess Ghyka, who owned the Villa Gamberaia and was responsible for the creation of the water parterre; the drawing may have been done to win favor, and jobs, from de Wolfe. Drawn by Pinsent in 1911, this plan of Villa Gamberaia was likely clear in his mind while preparing the drawings for Le Balze. In his 1931 article "Giardini moderni all'italiana," Pinsent presents an analysis of the ideal garden layout for modern times, supported by two of his own garden drawings. But he sees the ideal format most clearly demonstrated in the plan of Villa Gamberaia, with which he illustrates the text:

> The individual areas of the modern private garden should be small rather than large, and so more in harmony with modern life, which is more intimate than in the past . . . The modern garden is like the house laid open to the air, with rooms that when passed through provide a variety of impressions rather than having everything revealed at once. Passageways should be wide enough to allow a fleeting glimpse and to arouse the curiosity of those passing through the garden. The best example of this is to be seen at the Villa Gamberaia. Having walked around that garden, which is quite small in area, one goes away with the

impression of having spent more time there and of having discovered more levels than there are in reality.

This statement resonates with Mallows's advice that "the house plan must be extended beyond its walls, and include the

The series of garden spaces at Villa Le Balze, each transition marked by some form of arch and offering a distinct change of mood, from formal flower garden at the entrance to contemplative cloister. (Top, left, Pinsent's original sketch; photos Ethne Clarke)

Pinsent with with the Triton and decorations for the Le Balze baroque staircase, flanked by the craftsmen who created them, Signori Scheggi (left) and Toti (right), in August 1922.

entire garden scheme." The plan at Le Balze is such that the garden and villa are experienced sequentially as an enfilade of garden rooms with the villa at the center. The eastern end of the villa overlooks the so-called winter garden, a cloistered plan of formal beds centered on a circular basin fountain and overlooked by the loggia on the first floor of the villa as well as from an open loggia ranged along the northern side of the gardens. In Strong's day guests entered from this elevated loggia, so that their view of the property incorporated the villa, the cloister garden, and the distant view across the valley of the Arno; another entrance at street level, used by the disabled Strong, leads directly into the enclosed garden spaces at this end of the villa.

This primary passageway leads on past the cloister gardens across the northern façade of the villa, which faces into a nymphaeum, or grotto, part of a Baroque double staircase, decorated with busts of the philosophers Aristotle, Socrates, and Zeno and the orator Demosthenes, and crowned by a scrolled and a pedimented niche housing a statue of Venus supported by Triton.

All the *spugna* work in the garden was done to Pinsent's design and is an example of his learning a technique the better to show the workmen the effect he desired. In 1921 Pinsent wrote that to decorate the garden he had made two statues of river gods, two Hermes, and the four Greek portrait busts (one of whch is reputed to be Pinsent's self-portrait). The whole is framed by the double staircase that gives access from an upper level to the main entrance of the villa.

Visiting the Italian lakes with his family in 1910, Pinsent photographed the screen and decoration of the fountain court in the gardens of the Villa d'Este.

In his photo album dated 1910–1922, Pinsent leaves clear evidence of the source for the decoration of this intimate interlude in the garden's unfolding plan. The first pages are taken up with his photos of the balustrades, staircases, and screens at the Villa d'Este on Lake Como. Obelisks, busts, and masks in decorated medallions encrusted with pebble mosaics and *spugna* are carefully recorded alongside snapshots of the Pinsent family on a holiday visit. Such photographs are a form of sketching and were Pinsent's way of documenting the architectural shapes and decorative treatments that he knew would one day be useful in his own work as he shaped his own architectural vocabulary. Famil-

Pinsent's model for the staircase and retaining wall for the grotto at Le Balze, August 1919. The greatest drama is in the grotto passage; the grotto itself lies opposite the main entrance to the villa and at the midpoint of the garden plan.

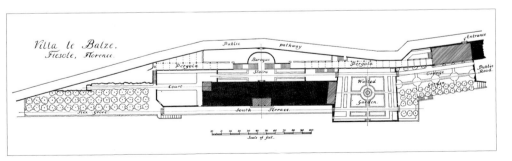

Pinsent's drawing of the plan for the garden at Villa Le Balze, dated August 1922.

The baroque staircase completed, except for the statue that will be placed in the niche, September 1922. Pinsent concludes the album dated 1910–1922 with these photos, just as he opened it with the photos of the exedra decoration at Villa d'Este, calling attention to the source of his inspiration for the Le Balze staircase.

The simple uncomplicated display of the library garden gives way to the small wooded grove; the tree trunks frame a view of Florence. (Ethne Clarke)

iarizing himself with the vernacular traditions and materials also made it easier for him to communicate with the local craftsmen, as he was speaking their artistic language as fluently as their spoken one.

The pathway through the garden eventually arrives at the library garden, ending finally in a small grove, or *bosco*, of live oaks. The trees of the *bosco* are set in a quincunx (a square with one tree at each corner and a fifth in the middle), which perfectly echoes the formality of the cloister gardens at the opposite end of the path, but without the ornate patterning of the parterre and the perfumed and colorful floral plantings. This complementary scheme ensures that the garden devolves gently from the disciplined architectural space of the street entrance into the natural landscape of the meadow and olive grove at the furthermost boundaries. This is a design element Pinsent included in his 1931 article: "At the boundaries of the garden we place woods and other more practical, less stylized elements." The secondary pathway runs parallel and leads directly across the open front of the villa with an unimpeded view of the valley below and the familiar outlines of the Duomo and Signoria on the Florentine skyline. With this simple treatment of open and enclosed spaces, Pinsent achieved the goal of creating a seemingly complex garden.

The garden spaces at Le Balze are individual enclosures, each possessing its own inward-looking character, a response to Strong's contemplative disposition. Strong's bedroom looks out in one direction across an uninterrupted view of Florence, and in the other down on to the walled cloister of the fountain garden. At the opposite end of the villa his library desk, raised on a shallow dais, faces into the austerely simple walled space of the library garden, which is enlivened only by a sparse lawn and a few simple shrubs. Pinsent's designs for Le Balze, therefore, provide not only a sympathetic environment, but a three-dimensional extension of his client's persona.

During World War II, the villa was commandeered by the German army as transport corps headquarters; the Allies attacked Le Balze in August 1944, and shelling caused major damage to the villa and its outlying structures. Pinsent, in his role with Allied Monuments Commission, was luckily on hand to advise on repairs, but from 1944 to 1980 it was unoccupied, although Margaret de Cuevas, Strong's daughter, retained a skeleton staff to ensure basic upkeep. In 1979 she made the villa over to Georgetown University, which has maintained it well as their center for Renaissance and Italian studies. In 1995 it was the venue for the first conference on Pinsent's life and work.

La Foce, Chianciano Terme

Of all of his projects, the one that gave Pinsent the most enduring pleasure, and stands today as the best testament to his values and beliefs as an architect and landscape designer, was the creation of the villa and gardens at La Foce, begun in 1924 for Iris Origo

(1902–1988), the daughter of Lady Sybil Cutting and her first husband, the American diplomat and banker William Bayard Cutting. In 1924 Iris was newly married to Marchese Antonio Origo.

Iris was brought up in the Anglo-American community in Fiesole and spent her early years in the graceful setting of the Villa Medici, her parents' home. When she and Pinsent first met, she was a lonely only child, and Cecil, eighteen years older, became like an older brother, investing their friendship with his experience of familial loyalty and affection. For Iris, by her account, the emotion was more intense, and she claimed to have fallen in love with Pinsent when she was seventeen, but was firmly rejected. Pinsent at thirty-five was unquestionably a handsome man, and he cut quite a dash in his portrait in uniform. Iris, whose youthful self-confidence was unsteady at best, may have regarded Pinsent as a safe target for her attentions. Mary Berenson, too, thought that Iris would be a suitable wife for Pinsent and sought to encourage him, but once again Pinsent found a polite but final way to say "no" to Mary's matchmaking efforts. So matters rested until one evening nearly a decade later, when both and Iris and Pinsent, having drunk too much, fell into a passionate embrace. Iris admitted that she had always had a strong physical attraction to Pinsent (her daughter Benedetta recalls Pinsent's sensual mouth as being his most memorable feature), but that evening they had not "technically" (Iris's word) become lovers. On his death nearly fifty years after their first meeting, Iris wrote to his relatives, "He was, I think, my oldest friend; all the memories of childhood are mingled with his," and she asked for Pinsent's slide rule as a memento.

In her autobiography, Iris described her first impressions on viewing La Foce, which at the time was a derelict property composed of a rustic coaching inn and a range of rundown outbuildings, set on the rise of low hill. The native landscape, the *Crete Senese* (Sienese clay), is the region of Tuscany south of Siena that takes its name from the rolling hills of predominantly clay soil. Centuries of cultivation have altered it from a fractured crust of stony crags and desolate scrub to a moonscape of rock-strewn fields accommodating the industrial agriculture patterns of southern Tuscany. Iris recalled: "[I stood] surrounded by these desolate hillocks: no tree, no patch of green, no trace of human habitation, except against the sky a half-ruined watch tower . . . Suddenly an overwhelming wave of longing came over me for the gentle, trim

Pinsent in army uniform, World War I.

Cartoon by Pinsent of Iris and Sybil Cutting bathing by the sea.

Florentine landscape of my childhood or for green English fields and big trees—and most of all, for a pretty house and garden to come home to in the evening. I felt the landscape around me to be alien, inhuman—built on a scale fit for demi-gods and giants, but not for us."

At La Foce, Pinsent realized his finest work as a modern humanist architect by redirecting the Origos' landscape from an unmanaged wilderness to one that was tamed into beauty and profitability. When the Origos arrived, the local *mezzadri* (the Italian equivalent of sharecroppers) were barely subsisting, riven

On a single page in the album dated 1923–1931, Pinsent (left) pasted this trio of images. He was at the height of his involvement with the Origos (above), and his relationship with Iris was developing in unexpected ways.

with disease and ignorance borne of nearly medieval superstition. The Origos' humanistic (and socialistic) ideals were brought to bear not just on transforming the property but also on improving the lives of the people who lived there.

Pinsent, collaborating closely with Iris and Antonio, began by fashioning the farmhouse into an elegant manor house in

The introduction of modernized farming was key to Origo's plan for success at La Foce, and plowing and draining the *crete* to make way for intensive cropping of wheat transformed the native landscape.

Pinsent and friend photographed standing in a field of high-yield wheat.

Iris and Antonio Origo inspecting the the work on a new road at La Foce, June 1935.

Antonio and Iris Origo among the flower beds in the lower garden at La Foce, June 1935.

the English tradition, surrounded by trim Florentine gardens of Pinsent's design filled with the flowers and grand trees of Iris's English vision. She filled the garden beds with sweet peas from the English seed merchants Sutton Seeds, annuals and perenni-

The La Foce estate as it appeared in May 1935.

View of the lower garden at La Foce. (Ethne Clarke)

als ordered from Thompson & Morgan, also in England, bulbs from van Tubergen in Holland, old-fashioned shrub roses, standard roses, and hybrid teas from Guillot in France, and irises from Monet's favorite nurseryman, Cayeaux. The formal beds of the upper garden nearest the house were to be planted with tulips growing out of forget-me-nots and schizanthus, hyacinths with pansies, and antirrhinums in vibrant color schemes for the spring. Summer plantings included dahlias and zinnias, pots of lilies and freesias, plumbago, and bougainvillea, while in autumn Japanese chrysanthemums were singled out. Iris's exuberant planting schemes—for they were most definitely hers since plants did not interest Pinsent apart from how they could be deployed in support of a garden plan—are typical of a first-time gardener who, suddenly finding herself with the blank slate of large new garden, rushes to fill it with all the plants her heart desires.

For Pinsent, the project offered more than just an opportunity to alter the physical topography; his long friendship with Iris meant that he was intimately aware of her emotional ties to

The view from the perimeter of the lower garden, looking up to the pergola walk, with the retaining wall of the grotto and double staircase to it along the right. (Ethne Clarke)

the gardens of her childhood spent in the elegant simplicity of Villa Medici. He drew on this heritage to help shape the mood of the place. As the plan evolved, the formal parterres, sunken nymphaeum, covered walkways, and enclosed gardens that huddle around the villa, sheltered from the outside world by thick screens of cypress and yew, reflect the Renaissance gardens of Iris's Italian upbringing as well as the inward-looking aspects of her personality. The more natural yet carefully managed parts of

The inner garden is a quiet and uncomplicated area, the first entered from the villa, and clearly influenced by Pinsent's early admiration of religious cloisters. (Ethne Clarke)

the landscape speak of her land-owning paternity and her need to belong, as well as of her desire to nurture a family and oversee the health, education, and general well-being of the La Foce "family" of workers for which she, as the Marchesa Origo, held central responsibility.

Pinsent stands edgily by among the supporting scaffolding of the grotto during its construction, 1955. (Courtesy of Benedetta Origo)

In the cloister-like inner garden, Iris enjoys the hundreds of spring tulips bursting forth froma an underplanting of annuals.

Pinsent's sensitivity to landscape and architectural space, along with his sympathetic response to Iris's needs, all come together at La Foce in a way that reflects their shared love of geometry and desire for orderliness, while also evoking their

In May 1935 the paths and lawns were edged with narrow floral ribbons.

The rugged gorse-covered crags of the Val d'Orcia's native landscape in June 1935 are thrown into sharp relief by the manicured cultivation of Iris Origo's flower-filled formal garden.

A view from the garden of the switchback style road. (Ethne Clarke)

individual emotional responses to this demanding site. Even the distant "alien, inhuman" landscape is brought into the garden by being framed and observed from carefully positioned viewpoints. In this way, the outward-looking elements of the design are brought under some degree of control. The most striking of these features is the road Pinsent laid out, which became the eye-catcher in the vista seen from a purposefully positioned seat in the wild garden behind the villa. This distant switchback road, lined with cypresses and umbrella pines, snakes up the hillside to a traditional Tuscan farmhouse. The Origos owned this property, and it was one of the first renovation projects Pinsent undertook for them, to provide sound housing for the estate workers. A road to the farm was essential, but although it may first and foremost have been a functional addition to the estate, there is no mistaking the artistry that went into its layout. This hard-working farm road is at the same time an eloquent reference to the underlying aesthetic of the entire La Foce estate that by its very existence tamed and mollified the harsh and demanding landscape of the Val d'Orcia.

The spacious entry arch to the La Foce *fattoria*. (Ethne Clarke)

Pinsent continued his work at La Foce until the mid-1930s, refining the garden and villa and designing and overseeing the construction of the estate's various working buildings, known collectively as the *fattoria*. His work extending and renovating these buildings is a testament to his knowledge of vernacular structures and evidence of his deep appreciation of how their architectural forms and motifs instill a sense of permanence and purpose to each new structure. By honoring the *fattoria* buildings' simple geometric forms but elaborating their dignity with details such as arches and window openings given generous, almost sensuous proportions, and repeating this throughout the compound, Pinsent created a clearly defined architectural language and identity for the entire La Foce estate.

This can be seen in two new structures Pinsent created for the Origos: a school building for the estate workers' children and what is ultimately the soul of the garden: a tiny cemetery and classical chapel designed by Pinsent as a memorial to the Origos' young son Gianni, who died in childhood. Anchored to its site by a sentinel oak tree, the chapel is located at the end of a path

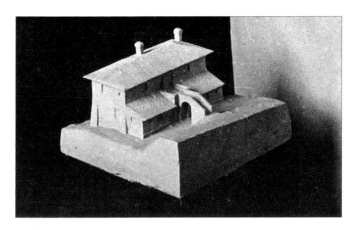

Pinsent's model for the La Foce estate workers' new school (top), and construction work under way, above, photographed in October 1934.

This photograph, taken in June 1935, shows Iris instructing the children on planting in the school garden.

which, winding along the hillside slope, links it with the formal gardens. Here the dynamic tensions of the built garden and its surrounding natural landscape are brought to the fore; stepping off the gravel path from the woodland one enters into an orderly, terraced memorial garden dominated by one of Pinsent's austerely devised chapels, where even the simplest elements of decoration are absent, leaving behind the pure geometric forms of classical

Clockwise from top, left: the pergola covered walk to the estate cemetery, the façade of the chapel in a Pinsent photo and today, and its interior, excellent examples of Pinsent's ability to return architectural form and space to its underlying simplicity. (lower right: Ethne Clarke)

architecture. Turning to exit, the path leads directly to the towering oak, its spreading crown so vast that it obscures even the vastness of the Val d'Orcia's spare landscape.

In the villa and garden at La Foce, as in no other, the ideal expression of the partnership between architecture and landscape

A stone polyhedron anchors the gently rising staircase in the main hall at La Foce.

The entrance court to La Foce. (Ethne Clarke)

For the mural in the dining room at La Foce, Pinsent created a number of imaginary landscapes that were then rendered by a local muralist. (Ethne Clarke)

is realized, as is Pinsent's obvious concern to establish mood and provoke an emotional response through a clearly defined yet personal language of architecture.

A visit to La Foce today shows that little has changed. The entrance to the drive is flanked by polyhedron-topped columns. (Are these a reference to Iris's love of geometry, or simply a traditional decorative theme? They have at least some thematic significance, because the polyhedrons appear as finials inside the villa on the main staircase.) Originally the road stretched directly across the building's entrance, but at La Foce, as at I Tatti, Pinsent relocated the road the better to accommodate a forecourt and automobile entrance as well as a main access to the *fattoria* area. Part of this ensemble is, of course, the entrance to the villa itself, but one that is so discreet, it is hard to locate. Hidden behind a dense little parterre and surrounded by an arbor, the steps lead into the villa hallway, the main dining area, living room, and other offices.

•

In addition to the expression of the client's personality and desires, in each of the gardens examined here a characteristic pattern can be discerned, and it establishes a rhythmic drama to the way in which each garden is experienced: expansive, outward-looking events of bold vistas are arrived at after a series of intimate, inward-looking spaces.

At I Tatti, the grand parterre terrace is reached and the distant view observed only after passing through the shadowy forecourt and *limonaia* building that virtually screens the vista. At Le Balze, the sudden revelation of the panoramic view of Florence is experienced after the progression of cloistered courtyards and grotto-like nymphaeum area. At La Foce, a sequence of flower-filled parterres, set like a sunken garden beneath a raised pergola walk, leads away from the villa's sheltered gardens to the parapet of a double staircase that rises above the sunken nymphaeum court. From this quarterdeck-like vantage point a panoramic view of the Val d'Orcia is revealed, a vista dramatized by the use of false perspective created from the lines of clipped hedges describing the parterre pattern of the sunken garden. From this configuration it becomes evident that when deploying architectural space within the landscape, Pinsent recognized the value of contrast and the notion of garden as theater, as well as the effect to be achieved by experiencing the areas of a garden "one by one."

On a recent visit to La Foce, this was brought home to me even more forcefully by something I had not noticed in previous visits. I climbed the hillside from the formal garden up to the small bench among the cypresses from where I had first viewed the little winding road on the opposite hillside. The bench was at the foot of a baroque statue that seemed to represent Africa, with the twisted, strained pose of the African's frame suggesting the raw energy and abundance of that once unknown continent. The path I had climbed was straight and each terrace reached was marked by a stone tread. My eye extended the line of the path across the valley to an end point in an expanse of untilled land-scape—a remnant, as Benedetta confirmed when I asked, of the original *crete senese*. I looked toward the fabled winding road: the line of view was along another garden path that was more natural,

One of the two main paths that ascend the hillside behind the villa, leading to vantage points from which to appreciate the gardens and the surrounding mix of agricultural and wild landscape. A perfect visual essay in Pinsent's recognized talent for "placing buildings in the landscape." (Ethne Clarke)

The stark and uncompromising landscape of the *crete senese* viewed between the overgrown cypresses lining the path on the terraced hillside behind the villa. (Ethne Clarke)

its subtle curves following the slope's undulations. Later, walking through the formal garden in the nymphaeum area, I found "Africa's" counterpart: a statue of a Caucasian youth (was it "Europe"?) crowning a stone bench designed by Pinsent as the focal point to the nymphaeum parterre's false perspective. Formal and informal, wild and tamed, tension and rest. Were these contrasting elements deliberately executed? Part of Pinsent's original plan? Perhaps. Whatever the answer, this configuration could be said to represent the humor and ingenuity evident in each of his designs. And Pinsent rarely did anything in his building or landscaping that was not deliberate.

Torre di Sopra and Gli Scafari

While La Foce was the apogee of Pinsent's career, other smaller projects were also on the boil, all for old friends, like the Italian sculptor Antonio Maraini and his wife, Yoï, for whom he designed the remodel of Torre di Sopra. Located south of the Boboli gardens, just outside the old city walls of Florence, the building was originally a *contadino*, or farmhouse, dating to the late eighteenth century. In 1926 the Marainis hired Pinsent to turn the farmhouse into a comfortable and up-to-date villa. In an article published in the *Architectural Review* in 1932, Yoï Maraini spoke highly of Pinsent's work there, writing that he had "remarkable knowledge, and most certain taste, in building modern houses that are in tradition with the best of Tuscan architecture." Part of her purpose may well have been to promote the interests of her old friend; she, Pinsent, and Scott had been part of the Berenson set before the war.

In her description of Pinsent's work on the conversion of the old farmhouse, she says that he left the exterior untouched and modified the interior with only the slightest structural alteration. He devised a hidden staircase to replace the old ladder-access to a tower room, while in the garden, his sensitivity to the needs of his clients and the building is evident in its placement within an appropriate landscape: "The garden is made by olive trees grow-

ing close up to the house, and everything has been done to preserve the surroundings as much as possible in keeping with the
simple beauty of a Tuscan farmhouse, still in its original setting."

•

After Sybil Cutting Scott and Percy Lubbock married, they retired to
a seaside villa on the coast at Lerici. It was named Gli Scafari, and Pinsent styled it after the Mediciean forts that dot the Tuscan coastline.

The driveway approach and entrance.

In 1929 Sybil Cutting and her new husband, Percy Lubbock, asked Pinsent to design a villa in the town of Lerici on the southwest coast of Tuscany. It was his final major project in Italy before he returned to England in 1935. The villa was situated on a rocky promontory that

Photographed in July 1931, the double loggia of the villa overlooked the promontory.

The lower loggia was outfitted as a soothing outdoor room.

stepped out into the sea; the rock face was pierced with caves and grottoes, and the impression of romantic wilderness could not have been more different than the setting of Villa Medici. As a place for two invalids to retire to, it was a bold and possibly unwise

In contrast to the formal gardens he was best known for, Pinsent, with Sybil and Percy, created a wild garden: here the daffodil walk in April 1934.

A watercolor, by an unknown painter, depicting Sybil in her garden.
(Courtesy of Benedetta Origo.)

choice. Iris remarked to her cousin Irene Lawley that although it was a place of great beauty, the austerity of the setting had the potential to make it joyless—a prophetic observation, as it turned out; Iris called the villa a "gilded cage," and although extremely beautiful—rose gardens twined with wisteria, and fountains played—it was not regarded as a happy home and visitors found it somber.

Pinsent, in characteristic form, set out to create a haven for his old friends. Construction began in 1931. The villa was named Gli Scafari, was itself understated, and rose quietly from the surrounding groves of olive and ilex. His reference here and at the villa Le Sabine he later fashioned for the Antinori family at Bolgheri was recognizably the Medici fortresses that dot this coastline, like the one at Forte dei Bibbona or dei Marmi. But where Le Sabine sits low behind a screen of pines among the dunes and just a few hundred yards from the beach, Gli Scafari rises up, commanding the shoreline. Both, however, sit firmly on broad bases, their sides battered upward toward low rooflines. In shaping the gardens, too, Pinsent acknowledged the setting, creating a wild

The villa for the Antinori family at Bolgheri.

garden of rose-lined paths and tumbling wisteria leading to the villa. Lemon trees in terra-cotta urns marked the drive. He later added a cloister garden to offer shelter from the salt-laden coastal winds, complete with pool and herbaceous borders.

Pinsent's sensitivity to landscape and his ability to shape his work according to its needs was one of his greatest design strengths. Today, when looking at the gardens and villas of Tuscany, we are seeing a largely reconstructed landscape, and as Giorgio Galletti has observed, "In thirty years [Pinsent] worked so intensively that one might say he partly redesigned two of the most famous hills of Florence, Fiesole and Arcetri." But he did so seemingly by stealth. Pinsent's work caused the least possible disturbance; he created areas of dignified spatial harmony closest to the house, while establishing the drama of disclosure with concealed vistas framed by shadowy hedge "walls" or "frivolous" flower gardens. And therein lies his success, as Galletti notes: "Pinsent had understood that the insertion of architecture within the Tuscan landscape was not a matter of camouflage, but of a continuous relation with the history of landscape."

•

While his final commissions were for memorials, Pinsent himself hasn't one. There is no grave on which to lay a sprig of bay or a rose from La Foce; today his only monument exists in the comfortable hillsides of Fiesole and Settignano and in the demanding slopes and clay fields of the Val d'Orcia, where he took the hopes and aspirations of his friends—for that is ultimately what his clients became—and shaped the landscape to them, leaving behind a picture that for visitors today, and the next generation of expatriates, shows the "true" Tuscany. But, as Henry James acknowledged in his essay "Florentine Notes" (1874), it is one shaped by a "sense of history . . . a mere tone in the air, a faint sigh in the breeze, a vague expression in things . . . Call it much or call it little, the ineffaceability of this deep stain of experience, it is the interest of old places and the bribe to the brooding analyst. Time has devoured the doers and their doings, but there still hangs about some effect of their passage. We can lay out parks

A pair of polyhedron-topped plinths frame the view of a landscape, imbued by nature with an infinity of graces, that enchanted and inspired Cecil Pinsent for more than thirty years of his architectural and garden design practice.

on virgin soil, and cause them to bristle with the most expensive importations, but we unfortunately can't scatter abroad again this seed of the eventual human soul of a place—that comes but in its time and takes too long to grow. There is nothing like it when it *has* come."

List of Clients and Projects

Source: "Index of Clients" prepared by Pinsent in 1955, courtesy Helen Morton. Project locations are in Italy unless otherwise noted.

Key to abbreviations:
A   Alterations /additions
D   Decoration
G   Garden
L   Library
N   New building

1908
Miss Jane Houghton; 20 St. Anthony's Road, Bournemouth, England; G: Small formal garden for new house.
Miss Jane Houghton; 20 St. Anthony's Road, Bournemouth, England; N: Medium house.

1910
Bernard Berenson; I Tatti, Settignano, Florence; A: Extensive alterations, including new library.
Charles Loeser; Villa Gattaia, Florence; A: Small alterations, layout of grounds.
Bernard Berenson; I Tatti, Settignano, Florence; G: Large formal park garden.
Bernard Berenson; I Tatti, Settignano, Florence; L: First library (large), to serve as sitting room.
Bernard Berenson; I Tatti, Settignano, Florence; N: Gardener's house.

1911
Lady Sybil (Lubbock) Cutting; Villa Medici, Fiesole, Florence; A: Alterations, sanitation, heating.
Bernard Berenson; I Tatti, Settignano, Florence; A: Alterations, extension and sanitation to Villino Corbignano.

Princess Mary Thurn und Taxis; Lautschin, Bohemia; A: *Servants' quarters in attic, stairs to library.*

Bernard Berenson; I Tatti, Settignano, Florence; D: *Free Venetian style decoration to ground floor salotto, in stucco, afterwards coloured.*

1912
Prof. Kiessling; Fiesole, Florence; A: *Alterations to villa.*

Prof. Kiessling; Fiesole, Florence; G: *Small terrace garden.*

Bernard Berenson; I Tatti, Settignano, Florence; L: *Second library (small).*

1913
Bernard Berenson; I Tatti, Settignano, Florence; A: *Extension for "Ritz" suite of rooms.*

C. A. Strong; Le Balze, Fiesole, Florence; N: *Large villa on hillside.*

1914
C. A. Strong; Le Balze, Fiesole, Florence; A: *Alterations to villino.*

C. A. Strong; Le Balze, Fiesole, Florence; G: *Formal garden on hillside.*

1915
Lady Sybil (Lubbock) Cutting; Villa Medici, Fiesole, Florence; G: *Layout of lower terrace and west terrace.*

Bernard Berenson; I Tatti, Settignano, Florence; L: *Third library (large), with recesses for study.*

1916
Bernard Berenson; I Tatti, Settignano, Florence; G: *West terrace garden, with baroque facade to library.*

1920
Charles Warrack; Florence; A: *Small alterations to villa.*

C. A. Strong; Le Balze, Fiesole, Florence; L: *Library to serve as study.*

1921
Lady Sybil (Lubbock) Scott; Villa Medici, Fiesole, Florence; L: *Red lacquer library with gilt ornament.*

1921–22
C. A. Strong; Le Balze, Fiesole, Florence; G: *Baroque garden stairs with sponge-stone sculptures and mosaics.*

1923
Edgar Davies; Borgo San Jacopo, Florence; A: *Alterations to apartment.*

Lady Sybil (Lubbock) Scott; Villa Medici, Fiesole, Florence; A: *Alterations to bedrooms on west side, etc.*

Mrs. Clarke; I Cancelli, Careggi, Florence; A: *Alterations to villa.*

1924
Marchesi A. and I. Origo; La Foce, Chianciano, Siena; A: *First alterations to villa.*

Mrs. Clarke; I Cancelli, Careggi, Florence; G: *Formal garden and garden stairs.*

Marchesi A. and I. Origo; La Foce, Chianciano, Siena; L: *Library, for use also as sitting room.*

1925

H. S. Whitaker; Villa Papiniano, S. Domenico, Florence; A: *Alterations to villa.*

Mrs. De Koven; Villa Imperialino, Foggio Imperiale, Florence; A: *Alterations.*

Miss Burnett; Florence; A: *Drainage and septic tank.*

F. W. Sargant; Via dell'Erta Canina, Florence; A: *Small alterations.*

Mrs. Harvey; Florence; A: *Small alterations.*

H. S. Whitaker; Villa Papiniano, S. Domenico, Florence; G: *Large formal garden in terraces.*

Sir George Sitwell; Montegufoni, near Florence; L: *Small "secret" library.*

1926

Countess Lutzow; Villa Bartolini, Florence; A: *Alterations to villa.*

Mrs. George Keppel; Villa Ombrellino, Bellosguardo, Florence; A: *New storey to wing.*

Mrs. Haslip; Villa Viviani, Settignano, Florence; A: *Small alterations.*

Miss Elizabeth Graham Frost; San Domenico, Florence; A: *New terraces.*

Mrs. Everett; "San Martino," Arcetri, Florence; A: *Alterations; buttressing of leaning facade.*

Mrs. Hayes Sadler; Villa degli Angeli, Fiesole, Florence; A: *Altar in chapel; garage.*

Antonio and Yöi Maraini; 6 Via Benedetto Castelli, Florence; A: *Conversion of contadino house into villa.*

Mrs. George Keppel; Villa Ombrellino, Bellosguardo, Florence; G: *"Union Jack" garden, with paths radiating like flag.*

Miss Nesta de Robeck; Florence; N: *Small villa.*

Mrs. Watkins; Via del Forte San Giorgio, Florence; N: *Medium sized villa.*

1927

Countess Lutzow; Villa Bartolini, Florence; A: *Further alterations.*

Harry Coster; Costa Scarpuccia, Florence; A: *New wing and corridor.*

Miss Harrison; Villa Bordoni, Florence; A: *Addition of living room.*

Duchessa Margaret di Melito; I Cancelli, Careggi, Florence; A: *Alterations: bedroom, bathroom, and servants' stairs.*

February 1926, Watkins: Garden and interior wall decoration for Mrs. Watkins.

Edward Vail; Villa Machiavelli, Maiano, Florence; A: *Alterations; porch.*

Countess Nora Khuen; Villa Spada, Rome; A: *Extensive alterations.*

H. S. Whitaker; Il Boccale, Antignano, Livorno; A: *Extensive alterations; reroofing.*

Comm. Traverso; Lungarno Amerigo Vespucci, Florence; D: *Wall frescoes to dining room, landscapes in baroque frames; chiaroscuro ceiling, and painted paneling to other rooms.*

Marchesi A. and I. Origo; La Foce, Chianciano, Siena; G: *Inner garden with fountain.*

Countess Nora Khuen; Villa Spada, Rome; G: *Box gardens and pond.*

Contessa Bossi Pucci; Montagnana, near Florence; G: *Part of garden.*

Lady Sybil Lubbock; Villa Medici, Fiesole, Florence; L: *Bookshelves for Percy Lubbock's study.*

Vincent Howells; Via delle Campora, Florence; N: *Medium sized villa.*

Miss Flora Priestley; Via delle Campora, Florence; N: *Medium sized villa.*

1928

Ernest Foster; Villa Colombaia, Via delle Campora, Florence; A: *Alterations to entrance and courtyard.*

Queen Sophie of Greece; 42 Via Bolognese, Florence; A: *Curing drainage smells.*

Mrs. George Keppel; Villa Ombrellino, Bellosguardo, Florence; A: *Room for Mrs. Trefusis, with decoration.*

Edward Bruce; Villa l'Orcio, Settignano, Florence; A: *New studio and loggia.*

H. S. Whitaker; Villa Papiniano, S. Domenico, Florence; A: *Further alterations.*

C. A. Strong; Le Balze, Fiesole, Florence; A: *Making service rooms in foundation floor.*

Harry Coster; Costa Scarpuccia, Florence; G: *Layout of terrace and pond.*

Lady Sybil Lubbock; Villa Medici, Fiesole, Florence; L: *Chapel converted into library.*

H. S. Whitaker; Il Boccale, Antignano, Livorno; N: *Garage and servants' house.*

Marchesi A. and I. Origo; La Foce, Chianciano, Siena; N: *Casa colonica (model).*

1929

Harry Coster; Costa Scarpuccia, Florence; A: *New cortile stairs, salotto, tower.*

Henry Clifford; Villa Capponi, Arcetri, Florence; A: *Sanitation and small alterations.*

Marchesi A. and I. Origo; La Foce, Chianciano, Siena; A: *Entrance gateway, screen walls, and pillars.*

Countess Lutzow; Villa Bartolini, Florence; A: *Rearrangement of guests' bedrooms.*

Mrs. Coletti Perucca; Villa all'Erta, Florence; A: *New porch and loggia; new cresting to garden facade.*

Marchesi A. and I. Origo; Villino Medici, Fiesole, Florence; A: *Extensive alterations and decoration.*

Marchesi A. and I. Origo; La Foce, Chianciano, Siena; D: *Wall frescoes to dining room, landscapes in, baroque setting.*

H. S. Whitaker; Il Boccale, Antignano, Livorno; N: *"Dopolavoro" building for village.*

1930

R. Blow; Villa Piazza Calda, Via di Piazza Calda, Florence; A: *New storey over servants' wing.*

Mrs. Dawes; Villa Passerini, Arcetri, Florence; A: *Making one large salon out of three rooms, etc.*

Dr. Roger Verity; Il Cicaleto, beyond Fiesole, Florence; A: *Alterations to villa.*

Marchese Uberto Strozzi; Palazzo Strozzi, P. del Duomo, Florence; A: *Reinforced concrete ceiling-terrace in cortile.*

Contessa Danoini de Sylva; Villa Giramonte, Florence; A: *Extensive alterations.*

Henry Clifford; Villa Capponi, Arcetri, Florence; A: *Alterations to villa.*

Marchese Uberto Strozzi; Palazzo Strozzi, P. del Duomo, Florence; D: *Baroque stucco decoration to bedroom.*

Marchesi A. and I. Origo; La Foce, Chianciano, Siena; G: *First extension of garden, box hedges, and flowers.*

Contessa Dandini de Sylva; Villa Giramonte, Florence; G: *Layout of terrace garden.*

Mrs. Coletti Perucca; Villa all'Erta, Florence; G: *Loggia, balustrades, and layout of terrace.*

Henry Clifford; Villa Capponi, Arcetri, Florence; G: *Enclosed terrace with bathing-pool and dolphins.*

1931

Marchesi A. and I. Origo; La Foce, Chianciano, Siena; A: *Alteration and decoration of ground floor sitting rooms.*

H. S. Whitaker; Lungarno Acciauoli, Florence; A: *Small alterations to apartment.*

Marchesa Margaret de Cuevas; Palazzo Strozzi, P. del Duomo, Florence; A: *Alteration and décoration of apartment.*

Signore Palchetti (plumber); Villino south of Siena; A: *Extension, end extra storey with loggia.*

R. Blow; Villa Piazza Calda, Via di Piazza Calda, Florence; A: *Alterations in villa; nurseries, etc.*

Lady Mackenzie; Villa Benivieni, Maiano, Florence; A: *Alterations to villa.*

Marchesi A. and I. Origo; La Foce, Chianciano, Siena; A: *Extension of fattoria forming courtyard.*

Henry Clifford; Villa Capponi, Arcetri, Florence; D: *Wall frescoes to bath room and toilet; landscapes - "Gentleman's Park".*

May 1931, Clifford: Pinsent designed the murals and fittings for Henry Clifford's resplendent bathroom at Villa Doccia (one of Edith Wharton's favorite places to stay, now the luxury hotel Villa Michelangelo in Fiesole).

August 1932, Spinola: Before and after Pinsent's addition of a dramatic mannerist façade for the old hillside villa and the addition of an elegant walled formal garden.

Dr. Roger Verity; Il Cicaleto, beyond Fiesole, Florence; G: *Pergola and garden.*

R. Blow; Villa Piazza Calda, Via di Piazza Calda, Florence; G: *Flower garden.*

R. Blow; Villa Piazza Calda, Via di Piazza Calda, Florence; N: *Studio building with apartment.*

Lady Sybil Lubbock; Gli Scafari, Lerici, Spezia; N: *Large villa on rock by sea.*

Marchesi A. and I. Origo; La Foce, Chianciano, Siena; N: *Storage building for fattoria.*

H. S. Whitaker; Il Boccale, Antignano, Livorno; N: *Port for motorboat, excavated in rock.*

1932

Lady Sybil Lubbock; Gli Scafari, Lerici, Spezia; A: *Alterations to hers and P's bedrooms and loggia.*

Marchesa Spinola (Formigli); Le Sorgenti, Quiesa, Lucca; A: *Alterations; enlivening of facade; entrance piazzale, etc.*

Marchesi A. and I. Origo; La Foce, Chianciano, Siena; A: *New suite of rooms for them on wing of villa; decorations.*

Mrs. Clifford; Villa Capponi, Arcetri, Florence; D: *Venetian rococo, décoration of bedroom in chiaroscuro; elaborate wardrobe also decorated.*

Lady Sybil Lubbock; Gli Scafari, Lerici, Spezia; G: *Flower garden near villino.*

Harry Coster; Costa Scarpuccia, Florence; L: *Library-study over church sacristy.*

Mrs. Coletti-Perucca; Castiglioncello, Livorno; N: *Large villa on rock-promontory by sea.*

1933

Baroness von Frisching; "San Martino," Arcetri, Florence; A: *Alterations to villa.*

July 1932, Coletti-Perucca: Villa at Castiglioncello, completed, christened "Godilanda"

Marchesi N. and C. Antinori; Villa Antinori, Scandicci, Florence; A: *Garage and wash-house; alterations to side facade.*

Henry Clifford; Villa Capponi, Arcetri, Florence; D: *Wall frescoes to bed room; elaborate Bibiena style architectural scenes in chiaroscuro architectural framework.*

F. Lawson Johnston; Fiesole, Florence; G: *Terracing and greenhouses for flower market-garden.*

Marchesa Spinola (Formigli); Le Sorgenti, Quiesa, Lucca; G: *Baroque courtyard and fountains, baroque lake, flower garden.*

R. Blow; Villa Piazza Calda, Via di Piazza Calda, Florence; G: *Complete formal garden and garden stairs.*

Marchesi N. and C. Antinori; Villa Antinori, Scandicci, Florence; G: *Flower garden; baroque screen; front to lemon-house.*

Henry Clifford; Villa Capponi, Arcetri, Florence; L: *Library with shaped crestings.*

Baroness von Frisching; "San Martino," Arcetri, Florence; L: *Small library.*

Marchesi A. and I. Origo; La Foce, Chianciano, Siena; N: *Garage building.*

Marchesi A. and I. Origo; La Foce, Chianciano, Siena; N: *Ambulatorio (first-aid clinic, with beds).*

Marchesi A. and I. Origo; La Foce, Chianciano, Siena; N: *Cemetery and chapel.*

1934

Princess Helen of Romania; Villa Sparta, S. Domenico, Florence; A: *Extensive alterations.*

Mrs. Coletti Perucca; Villa at Castglioncello, Livorno; A: *Addition of courtyard and covered way; access down to sea.*

Marchesi N. and C. Antinori; Villa Antinori, Scandicci, Florence; A: *Alterations to wing of villa to form large living room.*

Mrs. Dawes; Villa Passerini, Arcetri, Florence; G: *Garden, and lemon-house front.*

Princess Helen of Romania; Villa Sparta, S. Domenico, Florence; L: *Large library, used as main sitting room.*

1935

Princess Helen of Romania; Villa Sparta, S. Domenico, Florence; A: *Demolition of old staircase and construction of new.*

Marchesi A. and I. Origo; La Foce, Chianciano, Siena; A: *New altars and decoration of Castelluccio chapel.*

Lady Sybil Lubbock; Gli Scafari, Lerici, Spezia; A: *Alterations to villino with reduction of one storey.*

Mrs. George Keppel; Villa Ombrellino, Bellosguardo, Florence; A: *Extension to drawing room.*

Princess Helen of Romania; Villa Sparta, S. Domenico, Florence; G: *Part of garden.*

R. Blow; Villa Piazza Calda, Via di Piazza Calda, Florence; G: *Lemon-house, baroque stairs, and terrace.*

Marchesi N. and C. Antinori; Le Sabine, Bolgheri, Livorno; N: *Large villa on dunes by sea.*

Baroness De Frisching; Arcetri, Florence; N: *Studio building.*

Marchesi A. and I. Origo; La Foce, Chianciano, Siena; N: *Elementary School building.*

Marchesi A. and I. Origo; La Foce, Chianciano, Siena; N: *Infants' School building.*

1936

Mrs. Gomez-Haslip (Lally); Villa Viviani, Settignano, Florence; A: *Alterations to suite of rooms.*

Marchesi A. and I. Origo; La Foce, Chianciano, Siena; A: *Travertino paving to downstairs rooms.*

Signora Formigli (formerly Spinola); Le Sorgenti, Quiesa, Lucca; A: *Interior alterations, spiral stair, marble floors.*

Contessa Bossi Pucci; Apartment near Palazzo Serristori, Florence; A: *Plans for adaptation (carried out by them).*

Conte Giorgio de Chayes; Villa at Bagni di Lucca; A: *Extensive alterations.*

Marchesi A. and C. Antinori; Villa Antinori, Scandicci, Florence; A: *Extension of hall back towards garden.*

Conte Pandolfini; Villa di Tizzano, near Florence; G: *Layout of garden and piazzale.*

R. Blow; Villa Piazza Calda, Via di Piazza Calda, Florence; G: *Baroque grotto under garden stairs.*

Prince Paul of Yugoslavia; Brdo, near Kranj, Yugoslavia; G: *Baroque screen for garden.*

Baroness Traverso; Lungarno Amerigo Vespucci, Florence; L: *Small library.*

Marchesi A. and I. Origo; La Foce, Chianciano, Siena; N: *"Dopolavoro" building for contadini and labourers.*

1937

Marchesi N. and C. Antinori; Le Sabine, Bolgheri, Livorno; A: *Addition of rooms over garage.*

Myron Taylor; Villa Schifanoia, Via Boccaccio, S. Domenico; A: *Alterations; pond in garden.*

Lady Berkeley; San Lorenzo, Assisi; A: *Extensive alterations, heating, sanitation.*

Conte Gherardo della Gherardesca; S. Vincenzo, Livorno; A: *Plans for new stair-case (carried out by client).*

1938

Conte Rainieri della Gherardesca; Villa Margherita, Castagneto, Livorno; A: *Extensive alterations and additions (plans only); (carried out by client).*

H. S. Whitaker; Villa Papiniano, S. Domenico, Florence; A: *New chapel and staircase for access.*

King George of Greece; Tatoi, Athens, Greece; A: *Extensive alterations, modernization, and sanitation to Victorian villa.*

King George of Greece; Villa Mon Repos, Corfu, Greece; A: *Extensive alterations and sanitation; new gateway.*

Arthur Jeffress; Marwell House, Owslebury, near Winchester, England; G: *Large formal garden.*

Marchesi A. and I. Origo; La Foce, Chianciano, Siena; G: *Upper rose garden; new lemon-house and lemon garden.*

Signora Formigli (formerly Spinola); Le Sorgenti, Quiesa, Lucca; N: *Chapel with family tombs.*

Ralph Hamlyn; Burcott Farm, near Wing, England; N: *Medium sized house.*

1939

Signora Stucchi; Coltibuono near Montevarchi, Tuscany; A: *Plans for alterations (carried out by client).*

Signora Formigli (formerly Spinola); Fattoria "Adriano," near Volterra; A: *Plans for alterations (carried out by her).*

Signora Formigli (formerly Spinola); Fattoria "Limone" (Empire style), near Livorno; A: *Plans for alterations (carried out by her).*

Marchesi A. and I. Origo; La Foce, Chianciano, Siena; G: *Final extension of garden, with travertino stairs, grotto, pond, and stone bench with statue.*

King George of Greece; Tatoi, Athens, Greece; N: *Mausoleum for King Alexander and Queen Sophie.*

Athens Racing Club; Between Athens and Piraeus; N: *Royal Pavilion at Athens racecourse.*

1949

Contessa Flavia della Gherardesca; Bolgheri, Livorno; N: *Memorial tempietto-chapel to her husband.*

1950

Bernard Berenson; I Tatti, Settignano, Florence; L: *Storage extension for books (5th library), in two stories; (carried out by administrator).*

1951

Hon. Mrs. Colin Forbes Adam; Skipwith Hall, Selby, Yorkshire, England; G: *Shelter-garden, and gateway.*

Lady Berkeley; San Lorenzo, Assisi; N: *Chapel.*

1952

Marchesi A. and I. Origo; Villino Medici, Fiesole, Florence; A: *Restoration and alterations after war damage (work in charge of Inq. Formichi).*

Lady Berkeley; San Lorenzo, Assisi; L: *Smallish library.*

1955

Marchesi A. and I. Origo; Monte Savello 30, Rome; A: *Plans for adaptation of large apartment (carried out by Inq. Gentiloni).*

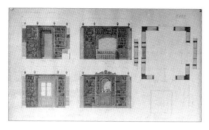

June, 1952, Origo: Drawings for the library at the *villino*, Villa Medici, Fiesole.

1956

Marchesi A. and I. Origo; La Foce, Chianciano, Siena; A: *Plans for conversion of office over garage into flat for new fattoria, with extension (carried out by Inq. del Consorzio).*

PROJECTS NOT CARRIED OUT

1910

Joseph Duveen; Place Vendôme, Paris; *Showroom for Italian works of art, for Paris showrooms.*

George Blumental; Ritz Hotel, Place Vendôme, Paris; *Scheme for adaptation of Spanish cortile for house in New York, and design for facade.*

1911

Arthur Acton; Villa on Via Bolognese, Florence; *Contadino house with baroque exterior.*

Princess Mary Thurn und Taxis; Castle of Duino, Gorizia (then Austria); *Decoration and ceiling schemes.*

R. R. Willson; Villa near Villa Gattaia, Florence; *Contadino house.*

1912

C. A. Strong; Fiesole, Florence; *First scheme for villa on site below Blue Nuns Convent.*

1914

Lady Agnew; Site near Ware, England; *Large house and formal garden.*

1916

Princess Mary Thurn und Taxis; Castle of Duino, Gorizia; *Small rococo chapel.*

December 1914, Agnew: Two views of a country house designed for Lady Agnew.

1923
Thornely Gibson; (Staying at Villino Corbignano, Settignano, Florence); *Large house with wings and music room, for England.*

1928
On. Roberto Franceschi; Angelo, near Montalcino; *Scheme for altering old house; scheme for new villa.*
Dottore Giglioli; Florence; *Design and model for villa by sea near Cecina, Livorno.*

1929
Mrs. Coletti Perucca; Villa all'Erta, Florence; *Scheme for large formal garden, with concealed tennis-court.*

1933
Signore Fummi; Rome; *Large villa for site on Via Latina.*

1937
Giorgio Uzielli; Villa Spada, Rome; *Elaborate formal garden with baroque features.*

1938
King George of Greece; Royal Palace, Athens; *Large villa with adjuncts, for site on slope of Mt. Parnes.*

1949
Queen Helen of Romania; Villa Sparta, S. Domenico, Florence; *Plans for conversion of contadino house into small villa.*

Cecil Pinsent, "Giardini moderni all'italiana"

ORDER AND SYMMETRY

The first characteristic of a garden in the Italian style is orderly symmetry. The modern stylized garden should have order and dignity in the area nearest to the house, so that the view from the window provides a calm and restful experience . . . At the boundaries of the garden we place woodlands and other more practical, less stylized [i.e., natural] elements.

GENERAL DESIGN

The individual areas of the modern private garden should be small rather than large and so more in harmony with modern life, which is more intimate than in the past. Large open spaces like those of French gardens are meant for gatherings of elegant gay people. The modern garden is like the house laid open to the air, with rooms that when passed through provide a variety of impressions rather than having everything revealed at once. Passageways should be wide enough to allow a fleeting glimpse and to arouse the curiosity of those passing through the garden. The best example of this is to be seen at the Villa Gamberaia.

ENCLOSURES

The height of hedges or masonry walls that surround various parts of the garden must be governed by the slope of the ground. [*In the accompanying designs a gentle slope to the south is imagined.*] As we have said, the purpose of the walls or enclosures is to conceal one element of the garden from another, exceptions being made for brief views that may be revealed along the way. To someone who is viewing the garden from the upper floors of the villa, the height of the walls should be such as to reveal the entire layout of the garden.

THE CHARACTERISTIC OF PERMANENCE

The second characteristic of a garden in the Italian style is that the main elements, be they materials or plants, that make up each section must give a sense of permanence, so that in summer and winter the structure of the garden will appear complete; seasonal plants should not be essential to the design of the garden. Flowers in bloom will enhance it somewhat, but the empty spaces left during the winter should not make the garden look like an unfinished project. For this reason, evergreen plants occupy an important position in the Italian-style garden. The purpose of flowers is to emphasize and add color to the design; flowering plants with luxuriant and spreading growth might disturb the architectural lines and should be avoided, although they would do very well in a flower garden. It is also advisable not to give to much space to flowers because their absence in winter would be too noticeable.

MOST SUITABLE PLANTS AND FLOWERS

Some evergreen plants, such as ilex, cypress, bay, box, and perhaps yew, are to be preferred for the perimeter of the garden, and magnolias and meddlers to give shade, because of the dignity and sense of order they provide and also because they may be easily cut into shapes suitable for different styles of garden. Pines, cedars, and conifers of irregular shape, and other trees, should be left to northern climates and their native mountains. In the same way, some flowers are preferable to others on account of their more uniform and contained mode of growth; they are therefore more easily framed and more suited to open spaces and borders of uniform color. As it is with opera singers, so it is with flowers in an Italian garden: the success of their art (and perhaps also their external appearance) depends on the success of the whole.

FOR FLOWER BEDS SURROUNDED BY BOX

Flowers that are to be placed in beds surrounded by small box hedges should be the most well-ordered, and it is advisable to choose them from a single species or variety and of a single color for each bed; only the taller flowers may be of a different color, but it must be harmonious or complementary.

In summer: wallflower, antirrhinum (medium and dwarf), godetia, petunias of a single color, and *Verbena venosa*.

In autumn: Lilliput asters and dwarf zinnias of different colors, dwarf dahlias or Japanese chrysanthemum in the form of a small tree.

It must be understood that to obtain a continuous succession of floral display, annuals must be sown in a seed bed and then transplanted to a pot-bed, and finally placed in the flower bed just before flowering.

Roses are not suitable in these small enclosures because of their slightly wayward growth. High-stemmed roses may be planted in corners, but in a row they disturb the architectural layout.

Designs using tall box, say from 50–70 cm [20–28 inches], are better without flowers; lawn is more suitable. Thus shade, which is one of the main beauties of these designs, can freely play upon it. If, however, flowers are desired, it is better to stick to small flowers like those listed above.

FOR THE BORDERS

In borders that run the length of a wall, scattered flowers may look very well. There are many varieties that are suitable as long as they are placed in large clumps or ribbons of one color and their growth habit resembles that of the flowers listed below. Flowers for the back of the border with a climber-covered wall as their background should be tall, but not more than one meter [39 inches] high, and their flower colors should harmonize with the climbers.

In spring the following flowers are advised: cheiranthus or wallflower, *Primula polyantha*, or buttercup, with small borders of perennial cottage pinks or violets.

In summer: lily, gladioli, iris, phlox, campanula (Canterbury Bells), delphinium, lavender, or rosemary.

In autumn: chrysanthemum, dahlia, zinnia, or aster.

Cosmea is an example of a flower that is not suitable because its growth is too loose.

Walls [or screens] of potted cypress or other greenery are better if they are finished at ground level with borders, and better still if they stand on a grass carpet.

FOR COVERING WALLS

Climbers on perimeter walls are allowed to grow more freely than those grown on walls behind borders. The winter season demands that at least a third of the wall surface be covered with evergreen climbing plants. They should never conceal the wall entirely, however, because it is pleasing to see patches of lichen-covered wall alternating with the greenery. There is no harm in climbers encroaching on the niches and panels of the walls if a particularly aggressive creeper damages a small part of the ornamentation when it is cut back. A garden can gain much from a slightly ruined air.

Among the evergreen creepers, ivy is the most invasive and its development should be forcefully restrained. *Ficus repens* also has the vice of growing invasively, but it may be freely cut back . . . Rhynchospermum is one of the most useful creepers because of its broad leaves and very subtle scent. The same is true of magnolias and oranges growing on an espalier, where the weather permits. Among deciduous varieties, any kind of climbing rose, jasmine, wisteria, or honeysuckle goes well among the evergreens. Climbing annuals such as convolvulus or clematis are more suited to a flower garden, because their tall thin stems are not conducive to the dignity of the stylized garden.

Notes

INTRODUCTION: NOTIONS OF ITALY

19 *Pinsent escorted many young architects*: See Marshall and Wallace, *Letters from Edward L. Ryerson European Traveling Fellows.*

19 *as Jellicoe described it*: Sir Geoffrey Jellicoe, interview by author.

20 *Edmund Houghton was a solicitor*: Jill Houghton, interview by author.

20 *Often the months abroad turned into years*: On one such expatriate, Lawrence Johnston, and the world-renowned garden he created in Gloucestershire, see Clarke, *Hidcote: The Making of a Garden.*

21 *Pinsent . . . carried the Italian-language edition*: Basil Pinsent to the author, July 1, 1995.

21 *"On the north side of the Arno . . ."*: James, *Italian Hours*, 241.

22 *the "infatuated alien"*: Quotations in this paragraph are from James, *Italian Hours*, 261.

22 *"Miss Paget has such a prodigious list"*: Edith Wharton to Sally Norton, March 17, 1903, Edith Wharton Collection (YCAL MSS 42), box 29, folder 897, Yale Collection of American Literature, Beinecke Rare Book and Manuscript Library, Yale University.

23 *"No one has your gift"*: Edith Wharton to Violet Paget, April 7, 1903, Vernon Lee Collection, Miller Library Special Collections, Colby College, Waterville, Maine.

23 *"where English boarding houses elbow . . ."*: Quoted in Pemble, *The Mediterranean Passion*, 41.

23 *"bands of swarthy gesticulating foreigners"*: Bradbury, *Dangerous Pilgrimages*, 165.

26 *discarded a portion of his possessions*: Allen Thomas, interview by author.

I. SHAPING A LANGUAGE OF DESIGN

27 *the Pinsent family maintained a position*: Basil Pinsent, interview by author.

29 *"a gloomy wonderland"*: Sir Christopher Pinsent to the author, April 26, 1991.

32 *At this time students were articled:* John Brandon Jones, interview by author.

32 *he was accepted as a student at the Royal Academy School:* Cecil Ross Pinsent, Candidate's Statement (Fellow), February 26, 1933, Library of the Royal Institute of British Architects, London (hereafter cited as Candidate's Statement).

33 *Hall's section drawings and floor plans:* "The London County Hall." In the copy in Pinsent's archive, one of the pages is annotated "Aug 1907" in his handwriting.

34 *"The moral [this book] is intended to point . . .":* Jackson, *Reason in Architecture,* viii.

34 *"hit the nail on the head . . .":* Blomfield, "On Architectural Education," 254.

35 *"the small but even then vigorous school":* Remaining quotations in this paragraph are from Williams-Ellis, *Architect Errant,* 66, 69.

41 *"for work put in hand when on tour":* Candidate's Statement.

41 *"Of the garden of Italy . . .":* Quotations in this paragraph are from Sedding, *Garden-craft Old and New,* 65, 93.

42 *Mallows's notes for this article:* C. E. Mallows papers, box 1, folder 2, MaC/1/2, Royal Institute of British Architects, London.

44 *described in* The Builder: "Design for Proposed Municipal Offices, Bournemouth," 620.

44 *"His work, as draftsman and architect . . .":* Davey, *Arts and Crafts Architecture,* 106.

2. ITALY: "HOW EDUCATING!"

45 *"Your dilemma reminds me . . .":* Pinsent to Basil Pinsent, March 14, 1935.

45 *Pinsent became engaged to Edmund's niece:* Jill Houghton, interview by author. William Weaver, in *A Legacy of Excellence,* incorrectly identifies Alice as the daughter of Edmund and Mary Houghton, likely based on Richard Dunn's first published paper on Geoffrey Scott ("An Architectural Partnership," 35). Dunn corrected the error in his later biography of Scott.

47 *"a true aesthete . . .":* Sir Geoffrey Jellicoe, interview by author.

49 *Basil Pinsent related:* Basil Pinsent, interview by author.

50 *"fetching me off the Palazzo . . .":* Pinsent to Bernard Berenson, September 7, 1953, Bernard and Mary Berenson Papers (1880–2002), Biblioteca Berenson, Villa I Tatti – The Harvard University Center for Italian Renaissance Studies (hereafter cited as Berenson Papers).

53 *"he developed into a real art":* Mariano, *Forty Years with Berenson,* 30–31. Houghton's photographs of Italian landscapes, shown to me by Jill Houghton, display his talent.

54 *The BBs:* This section draws on Strachey and Samuels, *Mary Berenson,* and Samuels, *Bernard Berenson: The Making of a Connoisseur.*

55 *"Here is the life to be lived . . .":* Strachey and Samuels, *Mary Berenson,* 41.

59 *"Berenson may know what's authentic . . .":* Quoted in Behrman, *Duveen,* 96.

59 *"We have had a young architect . . .":* Mary Berenson to Hannah Whittal

Smith, January 16, 1907, Hannah Whittal Smith Papers, Lilly Library, Indiana University, Bloomington (hereafter cited as HWS Papers).

3. CIRCLES OF INFLUENCE

62 *"could enjoy better health"*: Quotations in this paragraph are from Mary Berenson to Bernard Berenson, August 5, 1906, Berenson Papers.

63 *"as a very irrelevant and secondary sort of matter"*: Mary Berenson, diary entry, August 13, 1907, Berenson Papers.

64 *"I feel about as conscious as an oyster"*: Geoffrey Scott to Mary Berenson, January 15, 1908, Berenson Papers.

64 *"I get up in the morning . . ."*: Geoffrey Scott to Mary Berenson, February 19, 1908, Berenson Papers.

64 *Scott soon abandoned:* Dunn, *Geoffrey Scott and the Berenson Circle*, 66. Dunn writes that during this period Charles Reilly at the University of Liverpool asked Scott to assist in a course in general architecture, but this statement is undocumented and there is no mention of it in any of the other sources I consulted.

64 *"I shall be delighted to see Scott . . ."*: Bernard Berenson to Mary Berenson, April 2, 1908, Berenson Papers.

64 *"[Scott] is perhaps a little on my nerves . . ."*: Mary Berenson to Bernard Berenson, April 24, 1909, Berenson Papers.

65 *So it was that in 1909:* Mary Berenson to Bernard Berenson, April 20, 1909, Berenson Papers.

65 *Pinsent recalled that he was hired first:* Allen Thomas, interview by author.

65 *"Ours was a partnership of opposites . . ."*: Pinsent to Mary Berenson, undated (1911), Berenson Papers.

65 *"He gets up about noon . . ."*: Mary Berenson to Bernard Berenson, April 24, 1909.

67 *And he still had the idea of continuing:* Geoffrey Scott to Mary Berenson, c. October 1909, Berenson Papers.

67 *In March 1910 he was back in Florence:* Dunn, *Geoffrey Scott and the Berenson Circle*, 84.

68 *"hanging pictures"*: Mary Berenson to Bernard Berenson, October 11, 1910, Berenson Papers.

68 *Scott and Pinsent took an apartment:* Printed letterheads on Pinsent's stationery and later on stationery prepared for the partnership, now in the Berenson Papers, record his address changes.

68 *A six-page letter:* Pinsent to Mary Berenson, August 1911, Berenson Papers.

68 *"growing merrily"*: Pinsent to Mary Berenson, March 11, 1911, Berenson Papers.

68 *In a letter to her family:* Mary Berenson to Alys Russell and Logan Pearsall Smith, October 21, 1911, HWS Papers.

70 *Scott concentrated on writing:* Dunn, *Geoffrey Scott and the Berenson Circle*, 99.

70 *"Cecil works very hard . . ."*: Mary Berenson to Karin Costelloe, April 19, 1912, HWS Papers.

70 *"demolishing old aesthetic theories . . ."*: Arthur Balfour to Bernard Beren-

son, July 28, 1914, quoted in Dunn, *Geoffrey Scott and the Berenson Circle*, 136.

70 *"sponge-stone mosaics at BB's"*: Pinsent to Irene Lawley, February 15 (cont. February 24), 1916, Forbes-Adams Family collection, Hull History Centre, University of Hull (hereafter cited as Forbes-Adams Papers).

72 *"brooding through much of 1915 and 1916 . . ."*: Dunn, *Geoffrey Scott and the Berenson Circle*, 141–42.

72 *This question was temporarily answered*: Ibid., 160ff.

72 *"beloved Via delle Terme . . ."*: Pinsent to Irene Lawley, January 23, 1919, Forbes-Adams Papers.

73 *"the two most delicious nights . . ."*: Pinsent to Mary Berenson, September 3, 1913, Berenson Papers. On Fairfax, Beckett, and Rodin see Holroyd, *A Book of Secrets*.

74 *a clever little note*: Pinsent to Irene Lawley, December 12, 1912, Forbes-Adams Papers.

74 *"my old friends"*: Remaining quotations in this paragraph are from Pinsent to Irene Lawley, May 12, 1921, Forbes-Adams Papers.

75 *"[I had] set myself . . ."*: Ibid.

76 *a disastrous affair*: Quotations in this paragraph are from unpublished letters from Geoffrey Scott to Vita Sackville-West, dated between 1923 and 1925, in the collection of Nigel Nicolson, Sissinghurst Castle, Kent. I am grateful to Mr. Nicolson for allowing me access to this material. A full account of this devastating affair can be read in Victoria Glendenning's biography of Vita Sackville-West.

79 *"But what attracts me more than anything . . ."*: Pinsent to Mary Berenson, January 22, 1922, Berenson Papers.

80 *Pinsent marveled at Sitwell's requiring such an elaborate library*: John Brandon Jones, interview by author.

80 *"piece of writing paper on Scott's desk . . ."*: Watkin, foreword to *The Architecture of Humanism*, xv.

81 *Scott was hired by the American collector*: On this episode see Dunn, *Geoffrey Scott and the Berenson Circle*, chap. 16.

82 *the Order of George I, King of the Hellenes*: The medal is in the Pinsent archive.

83 *remarking to his family*: Basil Pinsent, interview by author.

83 *"What I have offered . . ."*: Pinsent to Mary Berenson, October 9, 1938, Berenson Papers.

83 *"But I couldn't somehow get back . . ."*: Pinsent to Bernard Berenson, September 21, 1941, Berenson Papers.

86 *"You brought to the solution . . ."*: Major N. T. Newton, A.C., to Pinsent, October 1, 1945, courtesy Helen Morton.

4. THE LAST FIVE SECONDS BEFORE MIDNIGHT

91 *"I feel no inclination . . ."*: Pinsent to Bernard Berenson, June 16, 1946, Berenson Papers.

91 *"It is nice to think . . ."*: This and the following quotation are from Pinsent to Bernard Berenson, March 20, 1946, Berenson Papers.

92 *"We are doomed . . ."*: Pinsent to Bernard Berenson, February 14, 1947, Berenson Papers.

93 *"we transcribe architecture . . ."*: Scott, *Architecture of Humanism*, 2nd ed., 213.

93 *At Villa le Balze in particular*: Shacklock, "A Philosopher's Garden," 77ff.

93 *"the architect models in space . . ."*: Scott, *Architecture of Humanism*, 2nd ed., 227.

94 *"Scott's powers of lucid exposition . . ."*: Clark, *The Gothic Revival*, 2nd ed., 2.

94 *"The slackness . . ."*: Pinsent to Bernard Berenson, January 8, 1948, Berenson Papers.

95 *"I was very interested . . ."*: John Brandon Jones, interview by author.

95 *"roused an interest in geology . . ."*: Quotations in this and the following paragraph are from Pinsent to Bernard Berenson, October 12, 1948, Berenson Papers.

96 *"Florence has a responsibility . . ."*: Bernard Berenson, "How to Rebuild Florence," unpublished manuscript dated April 17, 1945, box 1, folder 1, New Mexico D. H. Lawrence Fellowship Fund Collection, 1910–1960 (MS-3012), Harry Ransom Humanities Research Center Library, University of Texas, Austin.

97 *"the scenes of my most poignant experiences"*: Pinsent to Bernard Berenson, dated 1945, Berenson Papers.

97 Pinsent *"had really enjoyed being an architect . . ."*: John Fleming, interview by author.

97 *"The tempietto at Bolgheri looked harsh . . ."*: Pinsent to Bernard Berenson, June 2, 1949, Berenson Papers.

97 *"Time so often obliterates . . ."*: C. E. Mallows papers, box 1, folder 2, MaC/1/2, Royal Institute of British Architects, London.

100 *Pinsent quietly explained*: Luisa Vertova Nicolson, interview by author.

100 *"He was the first person . . ."*: Pinsent to Bernard Berenson, September 7, 1953, Berenson Papers.

100 *"I went to Italy with the Houghtons . . ."*: Basil Pinsent, interview by author.

100 *some discussion that he might live in Sheffield*: Chloe Morton, interview by author.

101 *a trip to the United States*: Ursula (Jane) Gibson, interview by author.

101 *"I cannot find anyone . . ."*: Pinsent to Bernard Berenson, March 1, 1953, Berenson Papers.

103 *"My life is not all calm . . ."*: Pinsent to Bernard Berenson, September 6, 1956, Berenson Papers.

105 *"I don't see why . . ."*: Pinsent to Bernard Berenson, December 19, 1954, Berenson Papers.

5. A SENSE OF THE INFORMING SPIRIT

107 *a country-house building boom*: See Crook, *Rise of the Nouveaux Riches*.

108 *"One of [Jekyll and Lutyens's] earliest masterpieces . . ."*: Ottewill, "Houses and Gardens in Britain," 7.

109 *Vincenzo Cazzato describes it*: Cazzato, "Restoration of Italian Gardens."

109 *"in its own right . . ."*: Neubauer, "The Garden Architecture of Cecil Pinsent," 47.

109 *"If the world is to make great gardens . . ."*: Sitwell, *On the Making of Gardens*, viii.

113 *a small house with formal gardens*: Pinsent, Candidate's Statement.

118 *Pinsent had good ideas for the new library:* Strachey and Samuels, *Mary Berenson,* 151.

119 *"He has strange periods . . .":* Mary Berenson to her family, January 18, 1913, HWS Papers.

121 *"I planted this avenue . . .":* Postcard from Pinsent to Mrs. Goddard, April 25, 1951, courtesy Helen Morton.

123 *"for giving so young . . .":* Mary Berenson to her family, December 19, 1910, Berenson Papers.

123 *"a dream,"* and *. . . clean and tidy "as a jewel":* Mary Berenson to Alys Russell, September 16, 1911, HWS Papers.

123 *"run on the rails of common sense":* Mary Berenson to Karin Costelloe, January 26, 1912, HWS Papers.

123 *"Cecil works very hard . . .":* Mary Berenson to Karin Costelloe, April 19, 1912, HWS Papers.

125 *"The elegance and grandeur of this house . . .":* Mary Berenson to Alys Russell, July 6, 1916, Berenson Papers.

125 *"imitation Baroque garden":* Clark, *Another Part of the Wood,* 163.

125 *Mary wrote to her sister Alys:* Strachey and Samuels, *Mary Berenson,* 265.

125 *"Although I had so gifted an architect . . .":* Berenson, *Sketch for a Self Portrait,* 133.

129 *"The designers [during the Renaissance] . . .":* Mallows, "Architectural Gardening," part 1, 181.

129 *"The individual areas . . .":* Pinsent, "Giardini moderni all'italiana," 69.

130 *"the house plan must be extended . . .":* Mallows, "Architectural Gardening," part 2, 31.

136 *"At the boundaries of the garden . . .":* Pinsent, "Giardini moderni all'italiana," 69.

136 *it was unoccupied:* Shacklock and Mason, "Survey and Investigation of a Twentieth-Century Italian Garden," 114.

137 *When she and Pinsent first met:* Origo, *Images and Shadows,* 115.

137 *by her account:* Moorehead, *Iris Origo,* 117–18.

137 *"He was, I think, my oldest friend":* Iris Origo to Chloe Morton, n.d., 1963, courtesy Helen Morton.

138 *"[I stood] surrounded . . .":* Origo, *Images and Shadows,* 211.

155 *"The garden is made by olive trees . . .":* Maraini, "The English Architect Abroad," 6–7.

159 *"gilded cage":* Quoted in Moorehead, *Iris Origo,* 151.

160 *"In thirty years . . .":* Galletti, "Il ritorno al modello classico."

Sources

INTERVIEWS

Sir Harold Acton. La Pietra, Florence, May 1990.

John Fleming (art historian). Villa Marchio, Lucca, July 1998.

Ursula (Jane) Gibson (Pinsent's neice). Telephone interview, 2003.

Jill Houghton (second cousin of Edmund Houghton). Walberswick, Suffolk, May 1995.

Sir Geoffrey Jellicoe (British landscape architect). Highgate, London, 1989; Ditchley Park, Oxford, 1990.

John Brandon Jones (English architect and authority on the Arts and Crafts period). Hampstead, London, September 1995.

Chloe Morton (Pinsent's niece). Various locations, 1991–1998.

Luisa Vertova Nicolson (former assistant to Bernard Berenson and librarian at I Tatti). Fiesole, Italy, June 1995.

Basil Pinsent (Pinsent's half-brother). Yaxham, Norfolk, several interviews conducted in 1993.

Allen Thomas (book and fine art dealer). Chelsea, London, May 1992.

BIBLIOGRAPHY

Behrman, S. N. *Duveen*. London: Hamish Hamilton, 1953.

Berenson, Bernard. *Rumour and Reflection, 1941–1944*. London: Constable, 1952.

———. *Sketch for a Self-Portrait*. London: Constable, 1949.

———. *Sunset and Twilight: From the Diaries, 1947–58*. London: Hamish Hamilton, 1964.

Blomfield, Reginald. *The Formal Garden in England*. 1892; London: Waterstone, 1985.

———. "On Architectural Education." *Journal of the Royal Institute of British Architects*, 3rd ser., 12, no. 25 (February 1905): 237–54.

Bowe, Patrick. "Designs on Tuscan Soil." *Country Life*, July 5, 1990, 91–95.

Bradbury, Malcolm. *Dangerous Pilgrimages: Transatlantic Mythologies and the Novel.* 1995; repr., London: Penguin, 1996.

Brooks, Michael W. *John Ruskin and Victorian Architecture.* 1987; London: Thames & Hudson, 1989.

Cazzato, Vincenzo. "The Restoration of Italian Gardens." In Fantoni, Flores, and Pfordresher, *Cecil Pinsent and His Gardens in Tuscany,* 91–117.

Clark, Kenneth. *Another Part of the Wood: A Self-Portrait.* London: John Murray, 1974.

———. *The Gothic Revival: An Essay in the History of Taste.* 1st ed., London: Constable, 1928; 2nd ed., London: Constable, 1950.

Clarke, Ethne. "A Biography of Cecil Ross Pinsent, 1884–1963." *Garden History: The Journal of the Garden History Society* 26, no. 2 (Winter 1998): 176–91.

———. "Cecil Pinsent: A Biography." In Fantoni, Flores, and Pfordresher, *Cecil Pinsent and His Gardens in Tuscany,* 15–32.

———. *The Gardens of Tuscany.* London: Weidenfeld & Nicolson, 1980.

———. *Hidcote: The Making of a Garden.* London: Michael Joseph, 1989; 2nd rev. ed., New York: W. W. Norton, 2009.

Crook, J. Mordaunt. *The Rise of the Nouveaux Riches: Style and Status in Victorian and Edwardian Architecture.* London: John Murray, 1999.

Davey, Peter. *Arts and Crafts Architecture: The Search for Earthly Paradise.* London: Architectural Press, 1980.

"Design for Proposed Municipal Offices, Bournemouth." *The Builder* 89, no. 3279 (December 9, 1905): 617–20.

Dunn, Richard, M. "An Architectural Partnership: Cecil Pinsent & Geoffrey Scott in Florence." In Fantoni, Flores, and Pfordresher, *Cecil Pinsent and His Gardens in Tuscany,* 33–50.

———. *Geoffrey Scott and the Berenson Circle: Literary and Aesthetic Life in the Early 20th Century.* Lewiston, Maine: Edwin Mellen, 1998.

Fantoni, Marcello, Heidi Flores, and John Pfordresher, eds. *Cecil Pinsent and His Gardens in Tuscany: Papers from the Symposium, Georgetown University, Villa Le Balze, Fiesole, 22 June 1995.* Florence: Edifer Edizioni Firenze, 1996.

Galletti, Giorgio. "A Record of the Works of Cecil Pinsent in Tuscany." In Fantoni, Flores, and Pfordresher, *Cecil Pinsent and His Gardens in Tuscany,* 51–69.

———. "Cecil Pinsent, architetto dell'umanesimo." In *Il giardino europeo del novecento 1900–1940: Atti del III colloquio internazionale, Pietrasanta, 27–28 settembre 1991,* ed. Alessandro Tagliolini, 183–205. Florence: Edifir, 1993.

———. "Il ritorno al modello classico: giardini anglofiorentini d'inizio secolo." In *Il giardino storico all'italiana [atti del convegno, Saint Vincent, Centro congressi del Grand Hotel Billia, 22–26 aprile 1991],* ed. Franceso Nuvolari, 77–85. Milan: Electa, 1992.

Glendenning, Victoria. *Vita: The Life of Vita Sackville-West.* London: Penguin, 1984.

Holroyd, Michael. *A Book of Secrets: Illegitimate Daughters, Absent Fathers.* New York: Farrar, Straus & Giroux, 2011.

Houghton, Mary. *In the Enemy's Country, Being the Diary of a Little Tour in Germany and Elsewhere during the Early Days of the War.* London: Chatto & Windus, 1915.

Jackson, Thomas Graham. *Reason in Architecture.* London: John Murray, 1906.

James, Henry. *Italian Hours*. 1909; London: Penguin, 1995.

Jekyll, Gertrude, and Lawrence Weaver. *Gardens for Small Country Houses*. 1911; London: Papermac Macmillan, 1983.

Lamberini, Daniela. "The Future of Cecil Pinsent's Garden Architecture and the Principles of Conservation." In Fantoni, Flores, and Pfordresher, *Cecil Pinsent and His Gardens in Tuscany*, 119–27.

"The London County Hall, Design by Edwin T. Hall, V.P., R.I.B.A., Architect." *Building News*, January 17, 1908.

Mallows, Charles Edward, and F. L. Griggs, illus. "Architectural Gardening, with Illustrations after Designs by C. E. Mallows, F.R.I.B.A." Part 1: *The Studio* 44 (September 1908): 181–87; Part 2: 45 (1909): 31–41; Part 3: 45 (1909): 180–88.

Maraini, Yöi. "The English Architect Abroad: A Tuscan Farmhouse." *Architectural Review* 71 (January 1932): 6–7.

Mariano, Nicky. *Forty Years with Berenson*. London: Hamish Hamilton, 1966.

Marshall, Lorne E., and George N. Wallace, eds. *Letters from Edward L. Ryerson European Traveling Fellows*. Lake Forest, Ill.: Foundation for Architecture and Landscape Architecture, 1931.

Masson, Georgina. *Italian Gardens*. London: Thames & Hudson, 1961.

Moorehead, Caroline. *Iris Origo, Marchesa of Val d'Orcia*. London: John Murray, 2000.

Neubauer, Erika. "The Garden Architecture of Cecil Pinsent." *Journal of Garden History* 3, no. 1 (January–March 1983): 35–48.

Origo, Benedetta. *La Foce: A Garden and Landscape in Tuscany*. Philadelphia: University of Pennsylvania Press, 2001.

Origo, Iris. *Images and Shadows: Part of a Life*. London: John Murray, 1970.

Ottewill, David. *The Edwardian Garden*. New Haven: Yale University Press, 1989.

———. "Houses and Gardens in Britain at the Turn of the Century." In Fantoni, Flores, and Pfordresher, *Cecil Pinsent and His Gardens in Tuscany*, 1–10.

Pemble, John. *The Mediterranean Passion: Victorians and Edwardians in the South*. Oxford: Oxford University Press, 1988.

Pinsent, Cecil. "Giardini moderni all'italiana, con i fiori che più vi si adattano." *Il giardino fiorito* 1, no. 5 (June 1931): 69–73.

Quest-Ritson, Charles. *The English Garden Abroad*. London: Viking Penguin, 1992.

Robinson, William. *The English Flower Garden*. London: John Murray, 1883.

———. *Garden Design and Architects' Gardens*. London: John Murray, 1892.

———. *The Wild Garden*. London: John Murray, 1870.

Ruskin, John. *Mornings in Florence: Being Simple Studies of Christian Art for English Travellers*. Orpington, U.K.: G. Allen, 1875–77.

———. *The Stones of Venice*. 1851–53; New York: Dover, 1989.

Samuels, Ernest. *Bernard Berenson: The Making of a Connoisseur*. Cambridge, Mass.: Belknap Press of Harvard University Press, 1979.

Scott, Geoffrey. *The Architecture of Humanism: A Study in the History of Taste*. 1914; 2nd ed., London: Constable, 1924.

Sedding, J. D. "About Modern Design." *The British Architect* 19 (March 16, 1883): 133–34.

———. *Garden-craft Old and New*. London: Kegan Paul, Trench, Trübner, 1895.

Shacklock, Vincent. "A Philosopher's Garden: Pinsent's Work for Charles Augustus Strong." In Fantoni, Flores, and Pfordresher, *Cecil Pinsent and His Gardens in Tuscany*, 71–90.

Shacklock, Vincent, and David Mason. "Survey and Investigation of a Twentieth Century Italian Garden." *Garden History: Journal of the Garden History Society* 23.1 (Summer 1995): 112–24.

Sitwell, George R. *On the Making of Gardens*. London: Gerald Duckworth & Sons, 1909.

Sprigge, Sylvia. *Berenson: A Biography*. London: George Allen & Unwin, 1960.

Strachey, Barbara, and Jayne Samuels, eds. *Mary Berenson: A Self-Portrait from Her Letters and Diaries*. London: Victor Gollancz, 1983.

Watkin, David. Foreword to *The Architecture of Humanism: A Study in the History of Taste*, by Geoffrey Scott. London: Architectural Press, 1980.

Watt, David, Vincent Shacklock, and Peter Swallow. "Conservation Advice in Tuscany." *Transactions of the Association for Studies in the Conservation of Historic Buildings* 18 (1993): 63–71.

Weaver, William. *A Legacy of Excellence: The Story of the Villa I Tatti*. New York: Henry N. Abrams, 1998.

Wharton, Edith. *Italian Backgrounds*. 1905; New York: Ecco Press, 1989.

———. *Italian Villas and Their Gardens*. New York: Century, 1904.

Wharton, Edith, and Ogden Codman. *The Decoration of Houses*. New York: Charles Scribner's Sons, 1897.

Williams-Ellis, Clough. *Architect Errant: The Autobiography of Clough Williams-Ellis*. London: Constable, 1971.

Index

[Page numbers in italic refer to captions.]